'The Leeming Light
Shines Bright . . .'

100 years of Mansfield's Palace Theatre
1910 - 2010

'The Leeming Light Shines Bright . . .'

100 years of Mansfield's Palace Theatre
1910 - 2010

Dedicated to the memory of Leslie Orton
1928 - 2007

Published by the
Old Mansfield Society
2010

© **Old Mansfield Society, 2010**
www.old-mansfield.org.uk

ISBN: 978-0-9517498-9-2

Compiled by the following members of the Old Mansfield Society:
Joan Piccini   John Vanags   David Crute   Pauline Ashton

With assistance from the Palace Theatre:
Andrew Tucker   Louise Atkin

WITH GRATEFUL THANKS TO THE MANY WHOSE CONTRIBUTIONS HAVE MADE THIS BOOK POSSIBLE.

Leslie Orton

Acknowledgements:-
Chad (including Mansfield Advertiser, Mansfield Chronicle, Mansfield Reporter,)
Mansfield Library
Mansfield Reporter
Nottingham Evening Post
The Weekly Post and Free Press

Old Mansfield Society Publications:-
'Mansfield in Old Photographs' - Old Mansfield Society.
'Mansfield a Pictorial History' - David Bradbury.
'Seats in All Parts' - Leslie Orton.

Contents

BUCKINGHAM PALACE

2nd September, 2009

Dear Mr. Tucker,

I have been asked to thank you for your kind letter about the Centenary of Mansfield Palace Theatre which is being celebrated in 2010.

Her Majesty was interested to learn about the theatre and appreciates your thoughtfulness in writing as you did. In return, The Queen sends her warm, good wishes to all concerned during this most special anniversary year.

Yours sincerely,

David Ryan
Director, Private Secretary's Office

Andrew Tucker, Esq.

Foreword

by

Tony Egginton, Executive Mayor.

I am delighted and proud to be in office at the turn of the Palace Theatre's Centenary celebration. The Theatre holds much affection in the hearts of the Mansfield district folk and over the years has provided many happy moments (be that as performer or audience member) that have endured with warmth through the lives of those touched by the venue on Leeming Street. Indeed times spent at the Palace – or the Civic as many people know it, evoke many memories of people who have spent time directing, performing and encouraging performances of amateur dramatics of our very own local grown talents. It has been "home" to some figures who are sadly now not with us who gave so much to encapsulate what the Palace is all about – the heart of the dramatic arts in Mansfield – names like Jack Tyler and Leslie Orton along with Michael Merry in recent years spring to mind. It is not just about the "localism" of the venue – but how it has played host to national and international stars – being a conduit for all the adoration and love that fans from Mansfield have exuded over artists like Ken Dodd.

The Palace is not just about bricks and mortar – though aesthetically it is a beautiful auditorium, of which I am justly proud. No, for me it's about the lives that the Theatre has touched and the hundred years of being the synthesis of adrenalin, excitement, entertainment and performance – about lines learned and costumes donned – it's about the human stories that make the Palace the venue it is - full of love and belonging to our community.

The human side of the Palace belies the positive impact it has on the Mansfield economy in business terms. The hard facts of running an entertainment venue is no easy task - I am sure that over the years the roller coaster of economic recessions and boom have taken their toll, challenging the viability of most provincial theatres; however, the Palace has stood the test of time, and so I pass on my thanks and congratulations to the staff, lead by Andrew Tucker (over the last few years) who has developed and worked with a passion to make the Palace Theatre the success it is.

On behalf of the people of the Mansfield District I congratulate and salute the Palace Theatre on its centenary and wish it well for the next 100 years!

PART ONE

THE PALACE ELECTRIC THEATRE
1910 -1930

Photo: A. S. Buxton 1903
Leeming Street from the corner of Bath Lane prior to the building of the Palace Theatre.

In the early years of the twentieth century almost all of the properties on the east side of Leeming Street were being sold for re-development. Alfred F. Houfton, a local building contractor, bought the plot next to the old Horse and Jockey (now ...andwhynot...) from the Sixth Duke of Portland. Mr. Houfton, who had worked on the construction of the Grand Theatre (now Riley's Snooker), paid £1,422 for the freehold site, planning to demolish the existing property and build an 'Electric Palace' which would offer the public moving pictures.

Moving pictures had reached the town as early as January 1879 with an exhibition at the Town Hall; there were further shows over the next few years. In 1905, the Hippodrome on Midworth Street (site of present day Gala Bingo) showed Biograph Pictures, along with live variety and circus acts. From about 1906, the Victoria Hall (later the Palais de Danse, now Q.I.) occasionally showed films.

As the twentieth century got underway, it became clear that cinematography was much more than a passing novelty. It had come to stay and its fast-growing popularity led to the construction of picture theatres in almost all towns of any size.

1

Legal and Public Notices.

PALACE ELECTRIC THEATRE
—————LEEMING STREET.—————

Proprietors: Manager:
PALACE ELECTRIC THEATRE Co.   MR. S. P. PECKOVER.
Telephone No. 212.

GRAND OPENING:
TUESDAY DECEMBER 13th,
AND EVERY EVENING AT 7-45 P.M.

Luxuriously Furnished and Decorated.
Comfortably Heated and Ventilated.

POPULAR PRICES:
Lower Pit, 3d.; Pit, 4d.; Pit Stalls, 6d.;
Grand Circle, 1s.

EARLY DOORS, OPEN 7 P.M.:
Lower Pit, 4d.; Pit, 6d.; Pit Stalls, 9d.;
Grand Circle, 1s. 3d.

Children's Matinee, Saturday Afternoon, at 2.30,
Admission: 1d. and 2d.; Adults as usual.

Seats may be reserved at Box Office, open from 10 a.m. till 3 p.m. or by
Telephone for Pit Stalls and Grand Circle at the same prices as Early Doors.
P.S.—Seats Reserved by Telephone NOT Guaranteed after 8 o'clock.
For the convenience of our Patrons, the Management have decided to issue
Books containing 10 Admission Tickets for Pit Stalls 4/-, and Grand Circle 8/-
These Tickets will be transferable, but not negotiable at Early Doors.

Original 'Grand Opening' announcement.

Dating from 1907, the Central Hall, Colne, Lancashire, is thought to have been the first purpose-built cinema in Britain. In 1910, the first purpose-built cinema in Mansfield would put the town well in the forefront of this latest trend in public entertainment.

Having studied other such Electric Palaces and striving to improve upon what he had seen, Mr. Houfton presented his plans to the Highways Committee who approved them without hesitation.

Aided by the architects, Messrs. Cook and Lane and teams of specialist craftsmen, work began in mid-July, 1910. Several local firms were employed; the electrical installations were carried out by the Mansfield Engineering Co. of Pelham Street, and the ornamental ironwork was by James Maude & Co. of Pelham Street. The painting, papering and gilding were under the supervision of Mr. C. E. Greenwood of Leeming Street, who had worked on the Grand and other theatres in Mansfield.

With both Mr. Houfton and his lessees, the United Electric Theatre Co. Ltd. of Piccadilly, London, being equally 'determined to give entertainment that would be worthy of the building', the whole project was completed in twenty-two weeks.

On the afternoon of Tuesday, December 13th 1910, in the presence of a large company of specially invited guests, the Mayor, Alderman Timothy Taylor J.P., officially opened the Palace Electric Theatre. 'With its imposing frontage in white ornamental plaster, it was considered a handsome and striking addition to the public buildings of the town.'

Photo: A. S. Buxton

Original frontage c.1920

The marble-floored vestibule, where the pay-box was situated, had two mahogany, brass-mounted, bevelled-glass entrance doors. The one on the right leading to the pit, the one on the left leading to the magnificently appointed lounge with comfortable chairs, rich carpets and a buffet, where light refreshments would be served. A handsome broad staircase led to the grand circle, while steps on either side led to the stalls.

The auditorium, believed to be one of the finest in the country, was 90 feet long, 45 feet wide and had excellent acoustics. It could accommodate 900 patrons in tip-up seats and was also provided with a piano and organ to accompany the moving, but silent, pictures.

The whole building was 'furnished and decorated in the most sumptuous and up-to-date plan, with that perfect harmony of colour which betrays real artistic taste'. The rich carpet of the lounge, grand circle and stalls and the whole of the seating was in electric blue. The walls, ceiling, circle front and proscenium were decorated with ornamental plaster painted in delicate shades and relieved with gold leaf. The electric globes were handsomely mounted and further embellished with dainty ruby hangings.

The parts the audience would not normally see were also of the latest and best quality. There were four large air pumps on the roof, to ensure the building was adequately ventilated. There was a concrete, fireproof generating room, which was lofty and electrically perfect. Two Kamm's Maltese Cross projectors had been installed. These gave an 18 foot picture, with an 85 foot throw. It was also planned to introduce the Cinephone, an early, but short-lived attempt to add sound to silent films by using a playback mechanism which, hopefully, synchronised the lip movements of the actors with a gramophone recording of their voices.

After the Mayor had declared the Palace open, 'a delightful cinematic entertainment' was given. Pictures depicting the Duke of Connaught (Queen Victoria's only surviving son) in South Africa and an Inspection of troops by the Khedive (Viceroy) in Cairo were remarkable for the vivid clearness and historical interest. An Italian drama was presented in a beautiful series of films and the chase and death of the poacher supplied both humour and pathos. Scenes at football matches, horse races and pictures of current events helped make up an event which was both interesting and educative.

During the procedures, Miss Gertrude Pegg sang with excellent effect 'Idle Words'. The report in the local press also added that 'the programme being both varied and extensive that even the most fastidious tastes could not but find something pleasing and acceptable'.

While promising to show the very latest and best pictures, the management also hinted that they had several innovations in view.

Mansfield Advertiser, February 24ᵗʰ 1911

Painting - Palace Foyer 1910

CHARLES EDWARD FLETCHER (1891 - 1995) - Employed by Barringer, Wallis & Manners, Rock Valley (1906-1961), Charles Fletcher created the original design for the Quality Street tin. As a freelance artist he painted portraits of dukes and princes across Europe.

From the very early days, together with the latest pictures - pathos, comedy, travel and drama - the audiences were also able to enjoy live entertainment - comedians, dancers, illusionists and ventriloquists.

Mansfield Advertiser, March 6th 1911

As the management proudly declared- 'Our Ambition is your Satisfaction - that's all.'

In January, 1913, Mr. A. F. Houfton, described in the official documents as 'carrying out the business of Electrical Theatre Proprietor' sold the Palace to the United Electric Theatre Co. Ltd.

Mansfield Advertiser, June 7th 1911

New owner and Manager

The First World War (1914-1918) brought huge numbers of soldiers into Clipstone Camp. As Mansfield was the nearest town for them to spend their off-duty hours, catering for their needs greatly boosted the economic as well as the social life of the town. Like all other places of entertainment, the Palace enjoyed four years of steady business, in spite of the introduction of an Entertainments Tax in 1916. With this, prices had to be adjusted and tickets were now sold with an 'Excise Revenue' stamp stuck to the back to prove the law was being obeyed. On the cheaper tickets, the new levy represented a high proportion of the total cost.

With the comparatively high audience figures during the war years the United Electric Theatre Co. Ltd. managed to keep afloat but they were clearly undergoing financial difficulties. When the Armistice was signed in 1918, they mortgaged their property for £4,750 to Albert Cahn of Nottingham. When Mr. Cahn died in 1922, his representatives sold out to William H. Percy, a Picture House proprietor of Kensington, London, who quickly sold it on to a couple of London Investment Syndicates.

In July 1923, the Palace Electric Theatre became the property of Sherwood Palaces Ltd. and on August 3rd 1923, the following announcement appeared in The Advertiser:

'The Palace Theatre in Leeming Street will be re-opened to the public on August Bank Holiday Monday. Extensive cleaning and many improvements have taken place and the arrangements being made for the comfort and entertainment of the public should be crowned with success. Owing to the short time at their disposal since taking over, the management have not had time to carry out all the improvements intended, but those made are undoubtedly on the right lines and will be appreciated by patrons. The best way for the public to decide is to pay a visit and judge for themselves. There seems to have been something missing in Leeming Street while the Palace has been closed and, as good entertainment at popular prices is beneficial to all, the re-opening of the Palace is a welcome addition to the town's social life. In addition to the principal features at each performance there will be high-class comedies, dramas &c., and the music will be of the best.'

The films, 'Jacques of the Silver North' (a six-reel drama), 'Uncle Tom Without his Cabin' (a two-reel comedy) and 'The Masked Rider' (a fifteen episode serial) were all released in 1919. They were all black and white, silent films.

This silence, however, was about to be broken. 'You ain't heard nothing yet' were the first words spoken on a film sound track when 'The Jazz Singer', starring Al Jolson, was released in 1927. It heralded an exciting new era in the film industry which soon made its mark in Mansfield.

The Grand Theatre took out a permanent cinema licence in January, 1929. In May it was re-named the Grand Super Cinema. At the end of 1930 it was taken over by Associated British Cinemas Ltd., who distributed the latest and best talking pictures. Although the stage was still used, films now predominated.

Also in 1929, the Empire Theatre, on the corner of Stockwell Gate and Rosemary Street, became part of the Gaumont Film Corporation. A sound system was installed and on December 16th, the first 100% talking movies were shown.

Photo - donated by June Webster (née Hibbert).
The staff of the Palace in the early 1920's. June Webster's mother, Phoebe Clarkstone, the third Chocolate Box lady on the right is standing next to her father, Marshall Hibbert, who was the projectionist.

On August Bank Holiday Monday, 1930, the new, luxurious and most modern Plaza Cinema on West Gate (Primark now occupies this site) opened with an 'all talking, singing and dancing' film called 'On With the Show'.

In 1910, the Palace Electric Theatre had been at the forefront of cinematic entertainment in Mansfield. Twenty years later it had lagged so far behind that it was struggling for survival. The management of Sherwood Palaces Ltd. had to face the stark reality of the situation. They clearly had only two options - either they closed down or they faced the opposition and moved with the times. Fortunately, they chose the latter.

PART TWO

THE PALACE (CINEMA & THEATRE)
1931-1949

FRIDAY, JANUARY 30, 1931.

=PALACE=

LEEMING STREET, MANSFIELD.

=TALKIES=

Commence Monday, Feb. 2nd.

Monday, February 2nd.
BEBE DANIELS
in 'Love Comes Along'
The All-Talking, Thrilling Drama with
Comedy, Song & Dancing.

Thursday, February 5th.
"RUNAWAY BRIDE"
Mary Astor & Lloyd Hughes
The All-Talking, Thrilling Romance of a
Dramatic Elopement.

MONDAY TO FRIDAY — — — — — CONTINUOUS FROM 6.
SATURDAYS AND HOLIDAYS — — — — TWICE NIGHTLY—6 and 8.15.

Mansfield Advertiser, January 30th 1931

Bebe Daniels and her husband Ben Lyon, later came to England and had great success with their television sit-com 'Life With the Lyons'.

The sound system, installed by the British Thomson-Houston Co. Ltd., reduced the seating to 800 but led to the proud boast that 'The Palace has the perfect sound'.

In spite of its lower ticket prices, the Palace faced stiff competition from other cinemas in the town, especially with the luxurious Plaza/Granada on West Gate. With its café providing dainty teas and morning coffee it proclaimed itself to be 'The Rendezvous of Mansfield' and as early as June 1931 was advertising a Warner Brothers' production of 'Hold Everything' - a musical comedy in Technicolor. From 1936, the mighty Wurlitzer organ was an added attraction for cinemagoers.

In general, two films were shown each week with a change of programme on Thursdays. Occasionally, as in September 1931, there would be a variation as shown. (*Page 10.*)

The Palace, as well as striving to keep up with its competitors, also had other problems. The fabric of the building was beginning to show its age. In 1937, pieces of the 1910 ornate plaster frontage began to fall off, creating a health and safety hazard. Plans submitted to the authorities asked permission for 'the modernisation of the front elevation' which merely resulted in the original frontage being replaced by plain rendering.

9

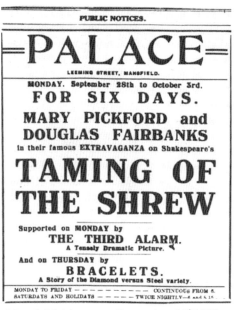

=PALACE=

LEEMING STREET, MANSFIELD.

MONDAY. September 28th to October 3rd.

FOR SIX DAYS.

MARY PICKFORD and DOUGLAS FAIRBANKS

In their famous EXTRAVAGANZA on Shakespeare's

TAMING OF THE SHREW

Supported on MONDAY by
THE THIRD ALARM.
A Tensely Dramatic Picture.

And on THURSDAY by
BRACELETS.
A Story of the Diamond versus Steel variety.

MONDAY TO FRIDAY — — — — — — — CONTINUOUS FROM 6.
SATURDAYS AND HOLIDAYS — — — — TWICE NIGHTLY—6 and 8.15

Mansfield Advertiser, September 25th 1931

The Kendall Family

From the mid-1930's and into the 1950's, the Palace was almost a second home to members of the Kendall family. George Kendall, Mansfield born and bred, veteran of World War I, became Commissionaire in the 1930's. He was also Manager for a while.

In his maroon uniform (buttons polished with Brasso) his peaked cap, white gloves and shining boots, he proudly stood on duty at the front of the Theatre which became his life.

At the children's Saturday matinee (the 'Tuppenny Rush'), his duties were of a slightly different nature, as the late Leslie Orton recalled:

'With George attempting to control us, we stampeded into the place. Being at the front of the queue ensured back seats, but the agony of waiting for the show to start! Saving places for pals was a dangerous tactic - George could spot an empty place in a packed house.' (Quote from article in Mansfield & Sutton Recorder, 2nd June 1986)

When out of uniform, George readily undertook other duties, often with the assistance of his young sons. He stoked the boilers. He trundled the variety artistes' luggage up to the station on a trolley borrowed from the Midland Railway. During the war he took his turn at Fire Watching on the roof. When this got boring he would do a spell of extra cleaning in the auditorium. Sometimes he would run errands, such as nipping next door to the 'Horse and Jockey' for a tot or two of whisky for one or other of the artistes.

Even when his working days at the Palace ended, George did not retire completely. During the holiday seasons he would go to Skegness to help out at the Arcadia, another of the Sherwood Palace's theatres. Members of the family would also go, to keep him company and give him a hand.

Photo - courtesy of Frank Kendall - 'Top Hat' 1936

George Kendall standing in the centre entrance.

Emmie, George's wife and mother of five, was always close at hand at the Palace. In the day-time she worked as a Cleaner; in the evenings she was an Usherette. As a child, Pamela, her younger daughter, often went with her during the day and, when she was old enough, she carried round the tray with ices and chocolates. Her other daughter, Joan, worked part-time, selling 'Eldorado' ice cream in the intervals.

From an early age, son Larry (known to all as 'Nip') also spent many hours at the Palace. Later, he worked there as a Stage-Hand, before being promoted to Stage Manager. He remembers how basic the under-stage dressing rooms were, but he never heard anyone complain.

His brother Frank also has vivid memories of youthful days spent at the Palace. On leaving school, in 1947, he got a day job as an errand-boy at Shentall's Grocer's on Regent Street. In the evenings he worked at the Theatre. On Wednesdays, Shentall's half-day closing, he did an afternoon matinee shift at the Palace. When it became a variety theatre, he helped with the lime-lights in the projection box, which was small and extremely hot.

Although much has changed on the intervening years, the remaining members of the Kendall family still feel great affection for the Palace.

As in the years of the 1914-18 conflict, the financial situation again improved during World War II (1939-45) when Mansfield, once more, became the entertainment centre for the many servicemen stationed in and around the town. From July 1940, Sunday opening of cinemas was allowed and this gave the troops more opportunity to enjoy their off-duty hours.

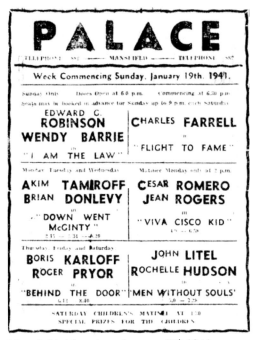

Mansfield Advertiser, January 17ᵗʰ 1941

The United States entered the war in December 1941 and in the following June the first United States Army Hospital in England was established at King's Mill. Until it closed, in April 1944, the American soldiers made their affluent presence felt in the town. Their pay was based on the cost of living in the States, which was higher than that in England.

During the war years there was no problem in obtaining films and cinemas were well patronised. They provided a warm, bright means of escapism from the more sombre realities of daily life, with its blackout, food rationing and often grim news from the war fronts.

Even though it was independent of the large film corporations which contracted the best films, Sherwood Palaces Ltd. felt confident enough to begin planning for the future.

In February 1944, they announced 'Children's Matinees are suspended until further notice'. In fact, the popular 'tuppenny rush' was never to return. The management had applied for a Stage Play Licence and Saturday afternoons were about to be put to a more profitable use.

Even before the licence was granted they staged live entertainment with the occasional week given over to films.

THE PALACE
LEEMING STREET, MANSFIELD. Tel. 882.

WEEK COMMENCING MONDAY, MARCH 13th.

GERALD MORRIS PRODUCTIONS PRESENT:

"VAUDEVILLE SNAPSHOTS"

A REVUSICAL ROAD SHOW FEATURING:

VINCENT RYAN
The Famous Australian
Comedian

DENISE VANE
Britain's No. 1 Glamour Girl.

ANNE WINTON
Variety's New Star.

PHYL D'OR
The Dancing Xylophonist

MONTY BIGGS
The Perfect Lady.

ARLETTE SISTERS
Setting the Pace.

VERNO & CASSELLI
The Tune a Minute Accordionists.

ALSO OUR RADIO COMPETITION.

CAN YOU BROADCAST?

CASH PRIZES £10.

The Palace Theatre Orchestra under the Direction of Frank Read

PLEASE NOTE:—MON. to FRI. ONCE NIGHTLY at 6.40 p.m.
SAT., TWO HOUSES at 5.40 and 7.45 p.m.
MATINEES, WED. and SAT. at 2.30 p.m.

Reserved Stalls 2/3.   Unreserved Stalls 1/6.   Circle 1/-.
Box Office Open at Theatre Daily at 10.30 a.m.

Mansfield Reporter, March 13th 1944

THE PALACE
LEEMING STREET, MANSFIELD. Tel. 882.

MONDAY, JULY 3rd, and Week.

STUPENDOUS RE-OPENING ATTRACTION
T.E.B Productions present

LOVE ON LEAVE

featuring
TOM E. BRADLEY
your favourite Comedian

Etta Selwyn   Joan Davis   Ken Wood

JILL JAYES   GLORIA LAVINE   EDITH COATES

Joe and Mervyn Whitehouse

Dorlornes Excelda Girls   Ida Johnson's Sunnybrooks

Mavis Lees   4 Hurricanes

MATT LEAMORE   Gloriana   **BILLY GIBBONS**
Light Comedian   A Foil for Tommy

Orchestra Stall 2/9 (reserved).   Stalls 2/3 (reserved).
Pit Stalls 1/6, un-numbered reserved.   Circle 1/-, unreserved.
Monday to Friday, Once Nightly, at 6.40 p.m.
Saturday, Twice Nightly, at 5.30 and 7.45 p.m.
Matinees, Wednesday and Saturday, at 2.30 p.m.
No half price.   All Children must be paid for.
Phone Bookings must be claimed 15 minutes before the
performance or they will be sold.
You are strongly advised to Book Early. No extra charge for
Booking. Box Office Open Daily from 10.30 a.m.

Mansfield Advertiser, July 3rd 1944

On April 24th they offered 'Showtime - a melange of music, mirth, and mystery with a host of stage and radio favourites'. On June 5th booked at enormous expense, they staged 'Blackpool Follies of 1944'.

The following week the Theatre closed for the fitting of fireproof curtains and other alterations in preparation for the Stage Licence, which was granted and due to come into effect from July 10th. The general public was informed that the Theatre would 're-open shortly with Revues, Road Shows, and Variety'.

Over the next months, this was followed by such shows as-
Piccadilly Scandals - with eight international nudes.
Fun and Dames of 1944 - American Burlesque Show.
Stage Door Scandals - the Newest, Fastest and Furiest Revue.

Throughout 1945 and until March 1946, the Palace continued this strong emphasis on 'Girls, Glamour and Laughter', with traditional pantomimes over the Christmas seasons and only on very rare occasions offering a serious dramatic play.

On March 11th 1946, after a production of 'Something Different - a new type of 'Road Show Revue', there was a strange lack of publicity in the local press until, under Public Notices on Sunday, June 30th 1946, it was announced that the Palace would open its doors for political reasons.

In 1945, the first post-war General Election had brought the Labour Party into power and as part of their Victory Conferences, Michael Foot, M.P. took to the Palace stage to explain his party's Foreign Affairs.

Labour's Victory Conferences

FOREIGN AFFAIRS

by

MICHAEL FOOT, M.P.

Member for Plymouth
World-famous Journalist

PALACE CINEMA

LEEMING STREET, MANSFIELD

Sunday, 30th June

6.30

Admission by Ticket only — 1/-

obtainable from the
LABOUR PARTY'S OFFICES
68 West Gate, Mansfield

Mansfield Advertiser, June 21ˢᵗ 1946

The year long press silence regarding theatrical productions was broken in March 1947.

In March 1947 the musical 'The New Companions' ran only from Thursday to Saturday, and the following week the Palace went back to films, one of them being in Technicolor before returning to musical variety shows presented by Eric Martin.

The next press announcement made by the management was 'Commencing Whit Monday - Important engagement of the Argosy Players under the personal direction of Miss Malyon Macaulay, presenting a season of West End plays'.

This Company came from one of the Sherwood Palace's theatres in Skegness and they were to stay in Mansfield from May 1947 until March 1949.

During this time, the Palace was often advertised as Mansfield's Repertory Theatre. With a new production every week the Argosy Players offered the public an amazing variety of plays, from classics, through murder and mystery, to comedy and farce.

One of the Argosy Players most notable productions was in November 1948 when, on a relatively small stage, they gave nine performances of G. B. Shaw's 'St. Joan' - with twenty-four artistes, fifty costumes, five suits of armour and six different changes of scenery!

Mansfield Advertiser, March 14th 1947

For two weeks, beginning March 7th 1949, the Company staged two plays - on Mondays, Tuesdays and Wednesdays playgoers could see 'Duet for Two Hands' and on Thursdays, Fridays and Saturdays they were offered 'Love's a Luxury'.

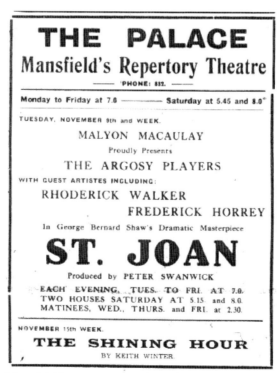

Mansfield Reporter, November 3rd 1948

These were their final productions. After ninety-five consecutive weeks in Mansfield, the Argosy Players took their final curtain.

15

ARGOSY PLAYERS LEAVE TOWN

The Argosy Players attracted big houses for the last three nights of their season and there was not a seat vacant for the final performance of "Love's a Luxury" on Saturday. John Evans received a terrific ovation when he first appeared in the role of "Mr. Mole."

Afterwards Malyon Macaulay thanked the public for their support over a period of nearly two years and said how sorry they were to be leaving. Mansfield would always have a warm spot in their hearts and they hoped, at some future date, to pay a return visit. From the wings she called Elizabeth White and, on behalf of the Players, wished her and Robert Weir good fortune on the occasion of their recent engagement. Robert Weir, who she said, had appeared more times than anyone else also spoke.

It took some time to distribute all the bouquets and gifts. John Evans received an armful and the biggest reception with Helen Cornwell a close runner-up. There was a special, uproarious, cheer for popular producer Peter Swanwick when he was presented with a bottle gaily decorated with vegetables.

Slowly the curtain was raised and lowered again and again and then . . . . . it came down for the last time for a few months.

Mansfield Reporter, March 18th 1949

The following week it was announced that the Palace would be:

'CLOSED UNTIL FURTHER NOTICE
for Complete Re-decorating and Re-fitting of the Theatre
in addition to Structural Alterations to greatly Increase
the Size of the Stage.'

This announcement appeared weekly in the local press for the next six months. Meanwhile, at the Theatre, the stage was made wider and deeper, the seating was reduced to 750 and three changing rooms were fitted out under the stage - these had hot water but no other facilities.

By September, and with a promise to present first class West End plays and musicals in the near future, the Palace was ready to open its doors again and a new era was about to begin.

PART THREE

THE PALACE THEATRE
(VARIETY, MUSIC HALL and REPERTORY)
1949-1954

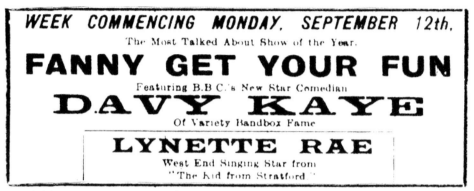

Mansfield Reporter, September 9th 1949

With this opening production, Sherwood Palaces Ltd. began to fulfil their promise of offering live entertainment to the theatregoers of Mansfield. It was followed by a series of other variety shows, including:

Mansfield Reporter, November 18th 1949

Topping the bill in 'Happiness Ahead' was Fred Brand, song and dance man usually billed as 'The Chocolate Drop from Dixie', although he originally came from Nottingham. Roy Castle considered him to be a genuine star, who greatly influenced his own work, particularly his tap dancing.

Aged seventeen when he appeared at the Palace, Roy Castle was already three years into his career as a much-loved, all-round entertainer, both in the theatre and on television. He is well-remembered as the presenter of the TV programme 'Record Breakers', which ran for twenty-two years.

Always involved in charity work, in 1992, after being diagnosed as having lung cancer, he began to work tirelessly to raise awareness of the disease and also to raise money for research into it. He was later awarded the O.B.E. for his services to show business and charity.

In January 1994, shortly before his death, he gave his name to the Roy Castle Fund, an appeal in aid of Cancer Research U.K. His wife, Fiona, herself awarded an O.B.E., is Patron of this fund which holds annual events to provide money for the fight against the disease which cut short the life of her multi-talented and much admired husband.

Fred Brand
&
Roy Castle

During the first months of following year, the entertainment offered to Palace audiences began to get ever more risqué. Typical examples were:

  'Sons of the Sea - the Naughtiest Scandals of 1950'.

  'Nudes are News - the most Sensational, Exotic, Daring Touring Show'.

  'French Capers - a Gay, Saucy Revue with a Continental Flavour'.

In spite of the 'naughty, exotic and saucy' flavour of these shows, reduced prices were offered for children from Monday to Friday! A fully-licensed bar was also now available as an added attraction for more mature audiences.

In February, 1950, came the 'Personal Appearance of 'Jane' of the Daily Mirror - the Living Cartoon Strip'. Accompanied by 'Mitzi', her dachshund, 'Jane' posed her way through the twelve months of the year in various stages of undress. Whether a thief really did break into the Palace and steal items of her scanty underwear is open to doubt. The same crime apparently occurred in other venues where 'Jane' appeared.

There was a complete change of mood in May 1950 when Frank H. Fortesque's Company opened another repertory season with Daphne Du Maurier's 'Rebecca'. Their final production in August was 'Is your Honeymoon really Necessary?'

Of their four month stay in Mansfield, the 'Reporter' commented:

'The company has ensured a regular weekly audience polished productions and consistently high-grade performances from all the actors and have aroused strong enthusiasm for the weekly 'rep'. Mansfield will be sorry to lose them.'

At the end of September the emphasis swung back to variety, headlining, among others, such well-known performers as:-

'The Crooning Blackbird' - Adelaide Hall. Comedians - Bunny Doyle, Stainless Stephen, Sid and Max Harrison and Johnny Lockwood, 'the Royal Command comedian.'

The Fraser Hayes Quartet appeared with Denny Dennis, who was billed as 'Britain's No.1 vocal star direct from his great tour of America where he featured with Tommy Dorsey's orchestra'.

On Sunday, October 22ⁿᵈ 1950, the Palace opened its doors for a more serious reason, to raise funds for a recent local colliery disaster. This tragedy happened in September, when friction from a jammed and damaged conveyor belt set it alight, trapping the night shift workers below ground. As a result, eighty men lost their lives. The people of Mansfield, many of whom were closely connected with the mining industry, quickly responded to appeals for help.

Mansfield Advertiser, October 20ᵗʰ 1950
Grand Celebrity Concert - Cresswell Colliery Disaster Fund.

19

On a much happier note, Arthur English, the 'Wide Boy', headed the bill in November 1950. Nip Kendall, then working as Stage Manager, remembers this very popular Cockney comedian coming off stage and asking 'Do that lot out there understand a word I'm saying?' The thunderous applause from the auditorium answered his question.

Arthur English

Shek Ben Ali

This show is also particularly vivid in the memory of Michael Bowler, a neighbour of the Kendall family and who, as a young boy, often went to the Palace with his mother. On this Monday night in November 1950, George Kendall stopped them at the door and asked if Michael would like to do a little job. This turned out to be acting as a stooge to Shek Ben Ali, one of the other 'seven tip-top acts' on the bill. When this 'Indian Illusionist' asked for a volunteer, Michael had to go up on stage and, as if by magic and to the amazement of the audience, Shek Ben Ali produced items which he had previously hidden about his stooge's person. Twelve-year old Michael went to every performance and was paid 5/- (25p) for his week's work.

From then on he became part of the Palace family, spending most of his free time there and doing all sorts of backstage jobs. On leaving school at the age of fifteen, he achieved his ambition of getting more permanent employment at the Palace. He was equally happy to be a stage-hand, working the flies moving backdrops or working the limelights. Unfortunately, only one year later, Michael was forced to revise his career plans and he eventually became a Master Baker. However, his connection with the Palace was not completely severed. He became involved in amateur dramatics and, in later years, stage-managed shows at the Palace, in aid of the Portland Training College and the Infantile Paralysis Fellowship.

In February 1951, Sherwood Palaces Ltd. leased the Palace to the Mansfield Palace Co. One of their first engagements was Michael Miles. He presented 'Radio Forfeits', a popular B.B.C. quiz show of that time, and later the game show 'Take Your Pick' with ITV.

In September 1950 Carroll Levis had made the first of his three visits to the town with 'his latest and greatest B.B.C. discoveries'. Compèred by Bob Andrews, this featured 'Betty Tye, Mansfield's Xylophone Queen' and 'Mansfield's sparkling personalities, Billy Koon and Molly Stuart - Laughter with Impressions'.

PALACE THEATRE
MANSFIELD

Lessees	THE MANSFIELD PALACE CO.
Booking Manager	BERNARD LANDO
Manager	F. GERALD CROSSLEY
Stage Manager	BILL HARRIS
Electrician	H. WHEATE

Telephones:

BOOKING OFFICE	882
MANAGER'S OFFICE	882
STAGE DOOR	2036

Programme heading showing new lessee.

A return visit was made in 1951, when the Canadian-born talent-scout presented the 'beautiful starlet' Violet Pretty who later, when she went into films, became better known as Anne Heywood.

Steve Conway, (1921-1952), like many other artistes of this era, was a familiar voice from B.B.C. radio shows such as 'Saturday Night Music Hall', 'Henry Hall's Guest Night' and 'Variety Bandbox'. Theatre audiences welcomed the chance to see their radio favourites live on stage.

The compère of this show was the late Barry Took, perhaps best remembered now as the presenter of the B.B.C. TV programme 'Points of View'. Earlier that year, the then twenty-three year old Barry had been interviewed by Carroll Levis, gone on to the finals of his radio show and wound up with a contract worth £12 a week. Barry then began a long career in B.B.C. radio and television as a scriptwriter, performer and presenter.

The 'Chronicle Advertiser' of April 5th 1951 noted that '**All star variety comes back next week, headed by a return visit of the popular young singing star of radio and recording fame, Steven (sic) Conway. After his successful début last September, packed houses are expected.**'

On April 30th 1951, 'Charlie's Antics - a sparkling revue' closed the season and on May 7th the Palace went back to Repertory when Weyman Mackay Productions Ltd. presented 'Easy Money - the Football Pool Comedy'.

By stark contrast, their next production 'No Room at the Inn' by Joan Temple, was based on the social problems of five children billeted by the authorities in an unsuitable house as there is no room elsewhere.

'No Room at the Inn' with Cynthia and Beryl on the sofa.

This was the first and last stage appearance of Beryl Burrows (née Knapp), although she was no stranger to the Palace. Her mother, Elsie, worked as a Cashier in the Ticket Office and later, for a short time, was Manageress. Gladys Cope, mother of her friend Tony, was employed as a Barmaid. Both Elsie and Gladys enjoyed their work and were avid collectors of photographs and autographs of the many artistes who appeared at the Theatre during this time.

The third Mansfield youngster in this play was twelve-year old Keith Kimberley who took over the role of 'Ronnie', the five-year old blitz orphan, at remarkably short notice.

The printed programme assigns the part of 'Ronnie' to Bernard Jewry, who later rose to stardom first as Shane Fenton of the Fentones and later as Alvin Stardust. In the event he was prevented from making his stage début in this play; it was strictly 'Adults Only', he was only eight years old and permission for him to take part was refused.

When Alvin was two years old, his parents moved from Muswell Hill, London and he spent his childhood and teenage years in Mansfield. The family lived in Clifton Place and his mother used their spare accommodation to take in 'theatricals' from the Palace. This meant that Alvin was surrounded by colourful stage people from an early age. On his way home from St. Peter's School, he often called in at the Theatre to watch rehearsals on the stage where he, himself, would later perform to enthusiastic audiences.

Bernard Jewry - at Junior School

Alvin Stardust

Week Commencing June 25th, 1951.

Weyman Mackay Productions
LIMITED

Presents

"PICK-UP GIRL"

by

ELSA SHELLEY

Judge Bentley	MAITLAND MOSS
Elizabeth Collins	BRENDA DEAN
Peter Marti	JAMES DRAKE
Mrs. Collins	IRENA CORCORAN
Larry Webster	HUBERT FORDE
Mrs. Marti	ROSE BEAUMONT
Mrs. Busch	GRAHAME FALCON
Mr. Collins	MICHAEL KEEFE
Policeman Owens	JAMES GILLEN
Ruby Lockwood	SHEILA MELBOURNE
Alexander Elliott	GEORGE WOOLLEY
Mr. Brill	WALTER PLINGE
Miss Porter	SALLY FORDE
Court Clerk	LESLIE ORTON

Play produced by GEORGE WOOLLEY

' PICK-UP GIRL' - cast list

The newspaper review of 'Pick-Up Girl' by Weyman Mackay Productions Ltd. says:

'Dealing with a subject which is often taboo, there is no gainsaying the moral impact upon the mind of the audience. The performers avoid any temptation to over-emphasise the salacious, without denying the realities of the evil. Leslie Orton, of the Mansfield Co-operative Theatre, is once again with the Company, in the role of the Clerk of the Court. Other local amateurs in the cast are James Gillen, (Policeman Owens) Peripatetic Teacher of Speech and Drama, Sheila Melbourne (Ruby Lockwood), another member of the Mansfield Co-operative Theatre and John Mail.'

George Woolley, who produced and acted in the play, was a professional actor and became a permanent member of the Company. He was born in Heanor and said he liked Mansfield audiences because they were his own people.

Weyman Mackay Productions ended their season on September 21st 1951, and under the direction of Tom Moss, the Palace began a prolonged season of variety shows, mainly of a 'saucy' nature and featuring less well-known artistes.

On October 15th when staging 'Just the Job' a new and novel 'Revuesical' - full of Colour, Music, Laughter and Song', the management announced:

**'PATRONS PLEASE NOTE
STARTLING REDUCTIONS IN PRICES
Variety at less than Cinema Prices
Mon. - to - Fri. Seats at 2/6, 2/-, 1/-
(Reductions for Children)'**

In December a show more suitable for family audiences was 'Happy Trails - packed with entertainment of a Western flavour'. This promised a personal appearance of Johnny Denis, with his famous horse 'Gunsmoke'. Valuable prizes were given away at each performance and children were admitted free if wearing any Western costume and accompanied by an adult. Even more spectacular and unusual, was the staging of Lucken's Circus.

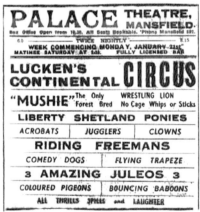

Mansfield Reporter, January 15th 1952

This was followed by more revues, ending on June 30th with 'Strip Show - a laughter show without compare' after which came another season of repertory presented by the Easedale Theatre Company.

The previous year, Janet Easedale had started her company in Darlington with her husband, Ottiwell Ingram, and her sister-in-law, Vera Ingram, as actor/producers.

In July 1953, the Easedale Players moved to Mansfield where, for the next five months, they entertained Palace audiences with a wide range of productions.

Josephine Tewson, straight from RADA, was with the players from its formation, happy to be paid £4.10s (£4.50) - a week for doing something she loved.

Ernest Ashley, Theatre Critic, writing of the Easedales production of 'Pick-Up Girl', 'Josephine Tewson once again proves her capability of taking on board any part offered and making the most of it. Miss Tewson should go far, and probably will.'

To promote the Company, Josephine remembers touring the Metal Box factory in Rock Valley and the Viyella-Clydella mill at Pleasley. She had a nightie from there, pieces of which are still in use as dusters.

Josephine Tewson

During her stay in Mansfield, Josephine shared digs on Sandy Lane with fellow-player, Maureen Coe. Their landlady provided breakfast and supper after the show. She also played her radio loudly on Sundays, their one day of rest when they had to do their laundry, learn their lines and try to relax.

After leaving Mansfield, Josephine stayed in 'rep' for several years after which, while still appearing on the stage, she began her television career - working with such well-known comedians as Charlie Drake, Dick Emery and Frankie Howerd. She often appeared with Ronnie Barker, particularly as his girl-friend in the six-episode series 'Clarence'. Then came 'Keeping Up Appearances', in which she played Elizabeth, Mrs. Bucket's (Patricia Routledge) nervous neighbour. More recently, in 'Last of the Summer Wine', she has been seen as the frustrated Librarian, Miss Davenport.

Josephine says her years in 'rep' gave her a solid foundation upon which to build her subsequent busy and varied career; an opportunity she fears is sadly lacking for the present generation of aspiring actors.

Noel Coward's 'Relative Values', presented in late November, marked the end of the Easedale Players' season in Mansfield.

The management noted that:-

'All play-lovers will be glad to know that a further series of plays is immediately to follow, commencing on Monday, December 7th. Please watch out for important announcement of the special attractions in store for your entertainment.'

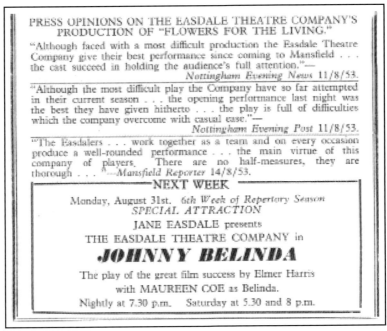

PRESS OPINIONS ON THE EASDALE THEATRE COMPANY'S PRODUCTION OF "FLOWERS FOR THE LIVING."

"Although faced with a most difficult production the Easdale Theatre Company give their best performance since coming to Mansfield . . . the cast succeed in holding the audience's full attention."—
Nottingham Evening News 11/8/53.

"Although the most difficult play the Company have so far attempted in their current season . . . the opening performance last night was the best they have given hitherto . . . the play is full of difficulties which the company overcome with casual ease."—
Nottingham Evening Post 11/8/53.

"The Easdalers . . . work together as a team and on every occasion produce a well-rounded performance . . . the main virtue of this company of players. There are no half-measures, they are thorough . . . "—*Mansfield Reporter* 14/8/53.

——NEXT WEEK——
Monday, August 31st. *6th Week of Repertory Season*
SPECIAL ATTRACTION
JANE EASDALE presents
THE EASDALE THEATRE COMPANY in
JOHNNY BELINDA
The play of the great film success by Elmer Harris
with MAUREEN COE as Belinda.
Nightly at 7.30 p.m.   Saturday at 5.30 and 8 p.m.

August 22st 1953

What followed was a short season of plays presented by Charles Sims and Co., including, on December 21st, - 'A Christmas Carol' which introduced pupils of the Gabrielle Osborne School of Dancing.

The year 1954 began with two pantomimes, the second of which was 'Cinderella' with 'Pip the Piglet' and 'a novelty new to pantomime and another favourite for the kiddies, the electric coach drawn by Shetland ponies.'

As usual, at this time, music was provided by the Palace Theatre's own orchestra, conducted by Tom Pitt, who lived in a caravan at the side of the Theatre. Animals also took centre-stage the following week when the 'Circus Rosaire' - brought along forest bred lions, performing bears, Royal Welsh ponies, monkeys and 'Goldie' the T.V. wonder horse.

Another series of musical revues included:

'You Must Not Touch' (March advertisment on following page.)

Later that month, Carroll Levis made his third visit to Mansfield and for the next four months offered patrons a series of revues with such titles as:-

'Taking off Tonight' - the saucy 'STRIP SHOW' which gives you bare skins and bikinis.

'Why Cover Girls?' - this'll make you whistle.

'Eve Goes Gay' - billed as 'an ideal family show' - a musical to suit all ages.

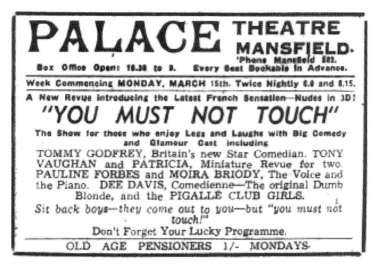

Mansfield Reporter, March 12th 1954

Early in July, there was a two-part show. Professional artistes entertained in the first half. After the interval, pupils of the Gabrielle Osborne School of Dancing introduced amateur artistes in a search-for-talent competition, with over £30 in prizes. This attracted over a hundred entrants - from singers and dancers to instrumentalists and acrobats. The contest was judged by 'audience applause' and the winner in the adult section was the Ernesco Trio, an acrobatic act from Staveley. The winner in the under-fourteen class was a song and dance act by three young ladies aged eight, nine and ten.

Advertised in the Mansfield Reporter of July 16th 1954, the revue 'Hot From Hollywood', which ran for two nights only, featured dancers, acrobats, trick cyclists, trampolinists, glamour girls and also the local talent competition prizewinners. A footnote to the advertising of this show read:

'From Monday next (July 19th) the theatre will be closed for renovation and cleaning. Re-opening Monday, August 18th, with new revue 'We Couldn't Wear Less.'

Jack Bradder, who had started coming to the Palace at a very early age, got a full-time job in a garage when he left school but, in 1953, he also began working part-time operating the limelights at the Theatre. His hours there were from five-thirty to midnight and he was paid £1.10s (£1.50) a week, plus tips from the artistes if he had made a good job of the lighting. He describes the job as being so fantastic he would have done it for nothing.

As with many others connected with the Palace, he recalls going across the road to Beecroft's Café, where entertainers and staff used to gather. They also met up with colleagues from the Grand and Granada and exchanged free passes for each others' shows.

Rosemary Varley worked at Beecroft's at this time and it was here that she met her future husband, Gilbert (Gilly), who was Stage Electrician at the Palace.

At the close of 'Hot From Hollywood', those employed at the Palace expected to have a month's break from their duties and were shocked when, just before August 18th they received letters telling them that the Theatre would be closed indefinitely.

Barny Lando, on behalf of the Mansfield Palace Company, lessees of the Theatre for the previous two and a half years, told the Mansfield Reporter, 'I do not know anything about the future plans of other people, but I am certainly not re-opening.' He also said that he had suggested making it into a cinema but the owners turned down the idea and, consequently, he had not taken up the option on the lease.

Mr. Gerry Crossley, the Manager, commented, **'This is most disappointing to all of us. We have tried to give the people everything from variety and revue to repertory. We have even had people coming from Nottingham, so perhaps it is Mansfield and district which does not want its own theatre.'**

According to the Reporter it was no secret that both Mr. Lando and the three repertory companies who had played seasons there had suffered heavy financial losses through poor support. Even with the return of variety, early in 1954, houses remained three parts empty, except at some special performances. The public, it seemed, were just not interested.

'It has always seemed to be a bit of a 'white elephant' for some reason,' one regular attender said when told the news. 'It seems an awful pity that a town of this size cannot support its own theatre.'

Added another, 'Perhaps there is a jinx on it. Or maybe it is the influence of television which has caused the decline.'

Most disappointed of all was George Kendall, 'It is the first time in twenty-five years I have handed in my keys,' he said regretfully. Throughout the time he had worked at the Palace, George had always been the first to arrive and the last to leave'.

'And so,' concluded Ernest Ashley of the Mansfield Reporter, 'another chapter in the chequered history of the cinema-cum-theatre has been written.'

This was undoubtedly true but although, for the next two years the stage remained dark and to the passerby the old Palace appeared to be abandoned, behind the scenes there was great activity. A whole new chapter was about to begin.

PART FOUR

THE CIVIC HALL
1956 - 1968

In August 1954, on learning that the owners had no future plans for the Palace, an article in the Mansfield Reporter posed the question: 'WAY NOW OPEN FOR CIVIC THEATRE?'

Rumours of this possibility had begun in the previous November and 'While quite a few prominent people agreed that something had been said about the idea and that it would be a highly desirable cultural addition to the town's amenities, the scheme had never got beyond that stage'. The article concluded that 'although the desire was there, no-one seemed willing to take the lead'.

However, unknown to many, the lead was being taken.

On April 14th 1955, only eight months after its closure, Mansfield Borough Council resolved to purchase the old Palace. By July, approval had been given to a plan which included interior and exterior alterations, provision of extra dressing and lavatory accommodation, as well as decorating and re-furnishing the premises. By the end of January 1956, arrangements were underway for the grand opening of what was to become the Civic Hall.

Chad, March 1st 1956

An invited audience of members of the Corporation and representatives of Borough organisations attended the first night. Old-age pensioners were guests at Tuesday's performance.

The Chronicle Advertiser commented on how 'the Palace Theatre had changed its inner face with coats of purple, stone, blue and gold paint, which had given the foyer and auditorium a contemporary air'. The total cost of this transformation was also revealed. The purchase price had been £11,500 and an additional £11,000 had been spent on the internal reconstruction and alterations. This latter sum had also included seating for 550, stage lighting, a film projector and a public address system.

In its Editorial column the local paper, while sincerely wishing the Civic Hall well, added 'Whether it will be worth the expense is something only the future will answer.' This expense caused great consternation among the taxpayers who had not previously been consulted and feared they would have to foot the bill.

The way in which the contracts had been allocated also caused controversy. The Chamber of Trade and Commerce reported it had received complaints from local retailers, electrical contractors, painters and decorators. They felt very strongly that, although they were more than competent to do the work, insufficient efforts had been made to ensure that goods and services were supplied by local firms and lucrative contracts had been placed outside the town. Carpets, to the value of £1,064 and seating, to the value of almost £2,200, had been supplied by Griffin and Spalding, Long Row, Nottingham (Debenhams now occupies this site). The electrical installations had been carried out by Messrs. Furse of Nottingham and the contract for painting and decoration had gone to a Sheffield firm. By contrast, dust covers had been bought from Frank Moss (now Eyres furniture store) of Toothill Lane, for the sum of £99 15s. 0d. (£99.75)

In late March, two members of the Civic Hall Committee admitted that they were aware of adverse criticism but re-affirmed that they wanted the Hall for the cultural and educational benefit of the town. The Town Clerk, Mr. A. C. Shepherd, said that although a general scale of charges had not been fixed, the terms notified to the five applications received were 7 guineas (£7.35) for morning and afternoon sessions of four hours and 10 guineas (£10.50) for evening sessions.

In answer to a question about the unfinished and untidy appearance of the frontage, the Committee was told that although, since the opening, satisfactory progress had been made internally, exterior alterations had not yet begun because it had not been decided what form they should take. Called a 'white elephant' by some disgruntled ratepayers, when the facade was painted later in the year, it was dubbed 'a yellow elephant'.

The first booking, after the opening week, was on Saturday, March 25th 1956 when a lecture was transferred from the Museum Lecture Hall (seating capacity 90) to the much more spacious accommodation now available at the Civic Hall. Here a capacity audience, who each bought a 1/- (5p) ticket, heard Sir Mortimer Wheeler give a lantern-slide lecture entitled 'Digging up the Past'.

Sir Mortimer was one of the best known archaeologists of the last century. In the 1950's he took part in three television shows, the most popular being 'Animal, Vegetable, Mineral?', which aimed at bringing archaeology to a much wider audience. In 1954, he was voted 'Television Personality of the Year'.

A month later, on Saturday, April 28th, and billed as the most important drama festival to be held in the town, the Divisional Final of the British Drama League's One-act Play Festival

Sir Mortimer Wheeler (1890 - 1976)

was held at the Civic Hall. The business and stage management arrangements were in the hands of members of local amateur groups. Leslie Orton, then with the Unity Players, was one of the Business Managers.

The Hall had three bookings in May. Brunts School, where Alderman Ethel Wainwright was Senior Mistress, held its prize-giving on the tenth. Three days later the Ethel Houseley Choir performed the concert version of 'The Tales of Hoffman' by Offenbach, with three professional singers taking the leading roles. Owing to the sudden illness of Miss Houseley, Mr. J. Domelow left the chorus to take over as Producer and Director.

At the end of the month, the yearly convention of Jehovah's Witnesses took over the Hall for four days and drew a large audience of delegates from thirteen Nottinghamshire Circuits.

In June the Mayor-elect, Mrs. Agnes Mitford, created a precedent by resolving to hold her traditional Sunday morning service in the Civic Hall. The vicar of St. Peter's Church said he was 'horrified' at the idea of holding an act of worship in an unconsecrated public hall. Major Parker of the Salvation Army, who was to be the new Mayor's chaplain, said that Mrs. Mitford's decision was irreversible and that many people had congratulated her on her choice.

In reporting the occasion, which took place on June 7th 1956, the Chad commented, **'Any fears that this year's Mayor's Sunday Service might be lacking in traditional ceremony were dispelled on Sunday, for the act of dedication conducted under the auspices of the Salvation Army at the Civic Hall for a congregation little short of five hundred, was marked by its reverent and dignified atmosphere.'**

Two Sundays later, when steady rain made the use of Carr Bank impossible for a Corporation sponsored Brass Band Contest, the event was hurriedly transferred to the Civic Hall. The new Mayor presented the awards, before a very sparse audience. Many fans had not been aware of the change in venue.

After being told by the Town Clerk that the Hall had been bought for local theatrical groups

31

and being urged to use it, Leslie Orton took this advice to heart. In June he presented the County Folk College's end of term 'Evening of Drama'; his own performance in one of the three plays being described as 'a remarkable tour de force'.

In July, the Civic Hall was the venue for a concert in aid of the St. John Ambulance building fund. Appearing before a three-hundred strong audience were the Osborne Starlets and the Rufford Colliery Glee Club.

A Grand Variety Show in aid of the Portland Training College for the Disabled was staged in October. This also featured local performers, who were supported by the Ravensdale Co-op Group, which presented 'Spotlight On Youth'.

Further proof that the town's amateur performers were beginning to take notice of the Civic Hall's advantages came in October, when the already well-established Penson Players made the first of their numerous appearances with the farcical comedy 'As Long as They're Happy'. There was scarcely an empty seat during the five-night production. Harry Penson, who had founded the group in 1948, described himself as 'speechless and breathless' when thanking the audience.

The Penson Players

The Penson Players, founded by Harry Penson, had already been in existence for nine years when the opening of the Civic Hall in 1956 enabled them to make use of the more spacious facilities now available in Mansfield. Following the outstanding success of 'As Long as They're Happy' they went on to stage one, and later two shows, offering their audiences a wide range of popular plays. At the age of seventy-four, after decades of acting, directing and writing plays, Harry retired to become President of the Company. For the next ten years, Peter Thistlethwaite, one of the original members, who designed, directed and acted, took over the leadership. Under his guidance the Penson Players went on from strength to strength.

The group was a member of the Nottingham and Nottinghamshire Drama Association (NANDA), which aimed to promote all aspects of amateur theatre arts and whose annual programme included competitions. Over the years, the Penson Players won many NANDA awards. They twice carried away the Newark Advertiser Shield for the Best Play of the Year; in 1970 for 'The Matchmaker' (directed by Harry) and in 1977 for 'Hay Fever' (directed by Peter). In 1979, Mrs. Thistlethwaite, who acted under her maiden name of Eileen Beale, won the trophy for best actress for her role in 'Relatively Speaking'. In the same year, and for the same play, her husband was awarded the trophy for best presentation, including scenery and costume. He was to win this five times in all. After Peter's retirement in 1982, the Penson Players' success continued both at the Civic and with NANDA. In 1984, they won the trophy for the group which had most effectively costumed its production. In 1973 they had donated the Harry Penson Rose Bowl, in memory of their founder. This was to be awarded to the best actor and was won, in 1989, by D. Pearce of the Penson Players. In this year they also gained the Newark Advertiser

PENSON
PLAYERS

present

"THE
FARMER'S
WIFE"

by EDEN PHILLPOTTS

THE CIVIC THEATRE
MANSFIELD

28th October to 2nd November
1968

CHARACTERS
(in order of their appearance)

ARAMINTA DENCH	EILEEN BALE
CHURDLES ASH	RON HARTSHORN
THIRZA TAPPER	JOY BARDEN
SAMUEL SWEETLAND	ERNEST BAILEY
SIBLEY SWEETLAND	MARGARET HIGGINSON
GEORGE SMERDON	KEN COX
PETRONELL SWEETLAND	SANDRA PARKER
RICHARD COAKER	ROGER PEARSON
LOUISA WINDEATT	JENNIE DAY
SUSAN MAINE	MARGARET NEWALL
SARAH SMERDON	MURIEL PEEL
BESSIE SMERDON	DIANE HASLAM
SOPHIE SMERDON	JANET HASLAM
VALIANT DUNNYBRIG	CHARLES BROWN
MRS. RUNDLE	JENNY GRIFFIN
DOCTOR RUNDLE	ROBERT WOOD
HENRY COAKER	MALCOLM SEYMOUR
MR. GREGSON	DAVID McLELLAN
MARY HEARN	SHEILA HASLAM
THE REV. TUDOR	GORDON PARTINGTON

THE PLAY PRODUCED AND THE SETTINGS DESIGNED BY
PETER THISTLETHWAITE
Construction by PETER THISTLETHWAITE, RON HARTSHORN
and other players

Copy of the Programme.

Shield for their production of 'Death Trap'. In 1992, Chris Keegan won the Best Actress trophy and, two years later, the group won the 'Front of House' award. Many well known and talented local actors drew in large audiences over Penson Players' forty-year association with the Theatre.

———————————————

Two other dates booked in October 1956 were for a Christian Scientist meeting and a Road Safety Exhibition with a quiz in which children from Mansfield and Sutton-in-Ashfield competed. The Sutton team won by a narrow margin.

Repertory fans were promised a short season (October 29th to November 24th) of popular plays under the auspices of Richmond Productions. Whereas only one week earlier crowds had flocked to see the Penson Players, Richmond Productions' first night at the Civic was deferred as only ten people turned up. On the Tuesday they played to an audience of fifty. At the end of the second week, Henry Richmond announced that the Council were not allowing his company to carry on and finish their season.

A more sizeable audience gathered on Sunday, November 11th, when the Mansfield Labour Party organised a public meeting to protest against the Conservative government's handling of the Suez Crisis. Speakers at this included George Brown, M.P. for Belper, George Deer, M.P. for Newark and Bernard Taylor, M.P. for Mansfield.

In October 1956, an uprising against the Communist regime in Hungary led to many Hungarians seeking refuge in other countries, including Great Britain. A considerable number made their way to Mansfield.

On Sunday, December 9th, the Salvation Army Band and Songster Brigade booked the Civic Hall for a musical evening in order to raise money for the Hungarian Refugee Fund. Tickets cost 3/6d (17½ p). A buffet and late transport were also offered to encourage the public to support this worthy cause.

A Holiday Travel Film Festival covered the weeks beginning October 26th and December 3rd. This gave a 1957 holiday preview, admission was free and each complete film show lasted approximately ninety minutes.

From New Year's Eve until January 11th 1957, pantomime returned to the Civic Hall with a professional production of 'Sinbad the Sailor' - reported to be 'a rattling good show'.

The Ethel Houseley Choir made its second appearance when they performed 'A Rebel Maid' before a large audience, on the evening of Saturday, January 20th. Two weeks later, to full-house notices, the Lorraine School of Dancing proudly presented its pupils' annual display. Jill Benson, who started dancing at the age of three, took part in this and thus began a close and continuing association with the Theatre.

During its first year, the Civic Hall provided ratepayers with several successful shows; some may have shown a profit and some definitely went on to become well-established annual events. There were, however, many weeks when it stood empty and unused - 'a mute monster' was how one Chad correspondent described it.

The second year continued in much the same way, with shows organised by local performers, the profits of which were donated to charity.

One of the most significant and successful events of 1957 was in April when, for the first time, the 'grande finale' of the four-day Mansfield Musical Festival was held at the Civic Hall. For the fifth successive year the distinction of highest marks awarded went to Miss Pamela Cook, who won the Council's Silver Rose Bowl.

David Chamberlain, then serving in the Nottinghamshire Constabulary, won the Edna Whitworth Cup and, for the third time, the Kent and Cooper Shield.

Both Pamela and David went on to play invaluable roles in the musical life of Mansfield and its Theatre.

Also during this year Leslie Orton directed the Westfield Folkhouse Players in 'On Monday Next', the Ethel Houseley Choir presented 'The Magnificent Faust' and the New Sheffield Symphony Orchestra gave a concert as part of the 'Music at Mansfield' programme sponsored by the Borough Council. The Penson Players, encouraged by their previous success, offered 'My Three Angels' to an appreciative audience.

In October 1957, Rex Mirfin Entertainments staged two evening variety shows which featured Larry Page, the recording star from the B.B.C. television programme '6-5 Special'.

Early in 1958, Holiday Travel once more booked the Theatre. Over three evenings, audiences could enjoy a free sound and colour film show which mainly featured holiday destinations in Europe.

Pupils of the Lorraine School of Dancing gave their annual display in February, with Irene Morley as the principal dancer.

In April, the Mansfield area heat of the County Youth Drama Festival, which had previously been held at High Oakham School, was transferred to the Civic Hall. The play presented by the Westfield Folkhouse Youth Centre, was once again judged to be the winning entry.

Early in May, after a considerable increase in entries, the Theatre was filled to capacity for the final concert of the Music and Drama Festival. This featured only the music section; the verse and drama sections were not included until May 1968.

Although the Portland Theatre, Sutton and the Festival Hall, Kirkby used the local press to advertise their live shows, there was very little advertising space given to coming events at the Civic Hall, except in the Public Notices Columns.

Chad, 1st May 1958

Ethel Houseley Choir

Ethel Houseley formed her choir in 1925. She retired in 1957 to become the Choir's consultant, allowing it to keep her name. Jack Domelow took over as Conductor and continued in this post for many years. Freda White, who had her own choir, was much in demand as an accompanist. Their annual Celebrity Concerts, became one of the traditional and popular events on the town's music scene until 1973, when after Miss Houseley's death, the Choir was wound down.

For three evenings in June, the Forest Players staged 'Separate Tables', in aid of the Old Age Pensioners' Building Fund and the Mansfield and District Spastics Club. This was their second major production since their formation in 1956.

In June, a correspondent to the Chad complained that the Civic Hall was still not fulfilling its full potential. Referring to it as 'our yellow elephant' he saw the danger of it becoming 'our forsaken elephant'.

Although, in 1959, the General Purposes Committee of the Borough Council did spend £250 on the repair and maintenance of the building and £142 12s. 6d. (£142. 62½) for the supplying and making of stage draperies and curtains, the 'yellow elephant' nickname was to continue until 1964 when, over a period of three months, the auditorium was redecorated and Theatre was given a 'new look' with the rebuilding of the foyer and the frontage.

Photo - J. W. Purdy 1964
This 'new look' included the removal of the original three arches.

However, 'forsaken elephant' it was not, at least on the part of the groups who had made their first appearances in the earlier years - the Ethel Houseley Choir, the Penson Players, the Forest Players, the Mansfield Music and Drama Festival - who continued to attract audiences to the Civic Hall over the following years. They were joined by other groups of actors, dancers and singers whose talent and enthusiasm demonstrated the wealth of ability which existed in the town. As the Town Clerk had said, 'We bought it for the use of the theatricals of our town. Use it.' And they did, with great success over the twelve years of the Civic Hall and beyond.

In 1958, under the auspices of the Westfield Folkhouse, Leslie Orton presented a revue, 'Request the Pleasure'. This was followed by the newly-formed Masque Players, making their début at the Theatre, in two more revues - 'The Pleasure is Ours' and 'Strictly for Pleasure'. (Their next revue 'This is it', in 1964, marked the opening of the 'new look' Civic.)

Tom Kettle and the Masque Players

Tom Kettle (Kett) actor, singer and dancer, was one of the early Associate Members of the Masque Players, formed by Leslie Orton in 1958, with the aim of presenting first class contemporary musical shows to Mansfield theatregoers. Other Founder and Associate Members, already well-known in local amateur dramatic circles, included Connie Orton, José Cooke, John Skinner, Peter Skinner, who was also the Scenic Designer, Sheila Melbourne, Ron Hallam, June Greaves, Freda Toft, Michael Merry and Shirley Winson. After spending ten years with the Masque Players, Andy Mulligan left to become a successful professional actor. He toured with Dora Bryan in 'Hello Dolly', did a six-month tour of the U.S.A. and Canada with The Royal Shakespeare Company (London) and spent three years in the original West End Production of 'Annie'. On television he has acted with such stars as David Jason and James Bolam. Another member, Derek Lewis, who was principally a dancer, went to New York and opened his own dance studio. The Players' choreographer was Irene Morley, who ran a local dancing school. Alan Gregson was the Musical Director. He played the piano and conducted the orchestra, usually made up of bass, guitar, percussion and woodwind.

The Masque Players were an independent group, with their rehearsal rooms at the Moot Hall (Market Place) and a scenery dock in Wood Street. Dora Bryan, star of stage, screen and television became their Honorary President. Patrons, booking from show to show, came not only from Mansfield and District but also in coach loads from much further afield. From 1959 onwards, Kett was involved in all the group's productions. Initially, they staged revues but in 1961 they presented their first full-length musical, 'The Boy Friend'. This was the Nottinghamshire Amateur Première, as was their April 1962 production of 'Kiss Me Kate'. In this, Kett was one of the 'gentlemen of the Company' and Jon Boden, an ex-miner, who had already become a professional singer, played the lead. Kett has happy memories of this show - from the message received from composer Cole Porter - 'My best wishes to you all'- to the cast's last night celebration dance and cabaret at the Cavendish Ballroom on West Gate. Leslie turned down an offer from the Manager of the Beatles to provide the cabaret because they were relatively unknown at this time. He opted, instead, for the Beverley Sisters and Jerry Desmonde.

Other Nottinghamshire Premières were 'Grab Me A Gondola' (1962), 'Salad Days' (1963), with Kett playing two small parts and understudying one of the other actors, and 'Guys and Dolls' (1964), in which he played 'Rusty Charlie'. Another memorable Nottinghamshire Première was 'Paint Your Wagon' (1964). In the opinion of the Chad Theatre Critic this show was 'an achievement of which not only the Masque Players, but Mansfield should be proud'. Lisa Skinner, daughter of José Cooke and John Skinner, at the age of six weeks, made her first stage appearance. Gwen, Kett's wife, took care of Lisa when she was not needed on-stage.

Several other Masque productions were also local amateur 'firsts' but 'Damn Yankees' (1965) topped this by being the British Amateur Première. Although some of the props were kindly supplied by an American Airforce base, the baseball outfits were made by members of the cast. Of the Spring 1967 production of 'The Music Man', in which Kett's two sons, David and Steven appeared, the Chad commented 'Honorary American Citizenship should be granted, if not to the whole Company, to the Director (Leslie Orton) and Designer (Peter

Skinner)'. 'The Secret Life of Walter Mitty' (Autumn 1967) led the Masque Players to even greater heights. It was the first time this musical had been presented in Great Britain by any company - professional or amateur.

THE MASQUE PLAYERS - President : MISS DORA BRYAN

presents

First performance in England
The British Premiere of

The Secret Life of Walter Mitty

— CAST —

WALTER MITTY	Ron Hallam
AGNES MITTY	Connie Orton
PENINNAH MITTY	Julie Littlewood
HARRY	Michael Merry
WILLA	Jose Cooke
IRVING KORNFELD	John Skinner
RUTHIE	Shirley Winson
FRED GORMAN	Peter Skinner
HAZEL	Pauline Hilton
SYLVIA	Kathleen Parsons

CAMEO ROLES played by

Pat Speed   Margaret Whyman   Harold Kettle   Peter Evans
Vilma Abbott   June Scholey   Alan Callaghan   Frank Sankey
Sheila Melbourne   Geoff Weaver   Albert Hopkinson
Terry Scattergood   Arthur Thorpe   Edward Stuart
Wilf Beaver   Barrie Tooth

DANCERS

Tony Redfern   Richard Crome   John Crome   Tony Bowsher
Margaret Porter   Christine Wallhead   Maureen Egerton
Shirley Winson   Pauline Hilton

Cast list of 'The Secret Life of Walter Mitty' 1967

The 1968 Spring production, and possibly their greatest triumph, was Lionel Bart's 'Oliver!', in which Kett worked backstage and Leslie played Fagin. Such was the demand for seats, that the six-day run had to be extended for a further three days. Boys from Meden School in Warsop, where Peter Skinner was Head of the Faculty of Art, joined the cast to play the workhouse lads and Fagin's gang. From May 13th -18th the musical was presented at the school. This made it the Masque Players' longest running show, with fifteen performances playing to a total audience of seven thousand.

Chad, 9th May 1968

Chad, 16th January 1969

In June, the whole company packed the show into a fleet of buses and took 'Oliver!' to Lichfield, where it was performed as part of the Midland's Musical Theatre Festival and where the boys won an award.

Other first-class musical successes followed - 'Little Me' (Midland's Première), 'Irma la Douce', 'Bye Bye Birdie' and 'Cabaret'. In April 1971 they presented 'It's Today' - a new, intimate revue, with lyrics and music written by members of the group - Paul Menzies, Michael Merry, Ron Hallam and Arthur Thorpe. In September 1971 it was announced that with 'Lock Up Your Daughters', after fourteen years and over twenty-five productions, the Masque Players would face their final curtain. The reason given for the decision to disband the group as reported in the 'Chad', was that rising costs had made it impossible to cover future productions at the box office, which was their only source of income. Ronald Parr, the Theatre Critic, wrote, **'It was hard to enjoy this show, knowing it was to be the last. This sad fact was underlined by an otherwise pleasing ceremony which took place after the**

39

first performance. Three members of the company, Arthur Thorpe, Ron Hallam and Leslie Orton, received long-service medals from the National Operatic and Dramatic Association'. The Kettles moved away from Mansfield for a number of years. Now back in their home town and, with Kett long retired from 'treading the boards', they are still keen patrons of the Palace; happy to sit out-front and enjoy the view from the other side of the footlights.

The staff and boys of Sherwood Hall School came to the Civic Hall in 1961, with Gilbert and Sullivan's, 'Ruddigore'. The guest artiste, in the role of 'Mad Margaret', was Sheila Haslam who, for the next ten years, continued to be a much appreciated guest artiste in the school's annual productions. From her earliest appearances as a competitor in the Musical Festival, Sheila went on to play an important part in the life of the Civic Hall, most significantly for her long, and continuing, association with the Cantamus Choir and the Music and Drama Festival.

Other amateur dramatic groups began to use the local Theatre at this time and their contributions were to span over many years.

Westfield Folkhouse Pantomimes

The Westfield Folkhouse group's first pantomime, 'Babes in the Wood' (1941), was staged in the W.W.I army hut from Clipstone Camp which stood beside the main building.

Arthur Froggatt was one of the players in this panto but, in future productions he preferred to stay backstage, gaining experience which served him well in the future. He joined the Penson Players at their formation in 1948 and was responsible for their lighting for many years. A very youthful Jack Tyler was another member of the thirty-plus cast of 'Babes in the Wood'. He and Ray Wallace played the two robbers.

Jack's cousin, Len Parker, was also involved in this first production. Len went on to specialise in playing the 'Dame'; this he did over the years, until 1985 when he made his last 'Dame' appearance in 'Jack and the Beanstalk'. Occasionally he varied his role, as in 1967 when 'he kept the audience laughing' as 'Lazy Larry' in 'Dick Whittington'. Ray Wallace, who played 'Idle Jack' in this panto, had by now become one of the long list of Folkhouse Panto producers.

The biggest turning point in the group's long history came in 1958, when the Borough Council invited the players to take advantage of the facilities now available at the newly- acquired Civic Hall. Jack Tyler, who was producing that year's pantomime, described the move as 'frightening' and was worried they would not be able to attract a big enough audience. His fears proved to be groundless. 'Red Riding Hood' was described in the Chad as an 'Outstanding Success', 'A Fabulous Comedy Panto' and a 'Show for the Whole Family'. Early booking was strongly advised. Originally planned to cover four evening shows, a request for two hundred tickets for the Saturday matinee resulted in an extra performance being hurriedly arranged.

During their years in the Folkhouse hut, the group would play to a capacity audience of around one hundred. By 1991, when they celebrated their fiftieth anniversary with a production of 'Cinderella', they were attracting audiences of over five hundred at the Civic.

One of the secrets of their success, as reported in the Chad (30th January 1991), 'is its close knit family structure. Many members are related to members from years gone by and many join when they are young and remain with the group when they become adults.'

Chris Ponka, Jack Tyler's nephew, who played 'Buttons' in 'Cinderella' began his acting career, aged four, as a cat. He made his first appearance at the Civic aged eleven and went on to play with every amateur drama group in Mansfield. After turning professional Chris made many T.V. appearances, including 'Brookside', and 'Doctor Who'.

Many other well-known amateur performers also took part in Folkhouse Panto's. In the 1950's, Josè Cooke played Principal Boy. In 'Cinderella' she played the 'Fairy Godmother'. Brian Stafford, who played with all the major groups in the area, also appeared in Folkhouse Panto's. Peter Skinner designed scenery, which was painted by members of the Youth Club. Over the years, Jill Benson's choreographic work has been greatly appreciated.

Les Pinder started working backstage, but then began to play comedy parts on stage. His first appearance was as the goose, 'Priscilla', in 'Mother Goose'. In the 1989 repeat production of 'Mother Goose' he played 'Idle Jack' and also co-produced this panto with Chris Ponka. He still continues to co-produce the annual shows and has worked with Tracy Wilkes and Christine Oscroft. Les is now on the Folkhouse Pantomime Committee. Other co-producers are Christine Oscroft and Brandon Stafford. David Gell is the Treasurer and Sally Ann Davis is Ticket Secretary.

As Les acknowledges, a very valuable contribution is, and always has been, made by volunteers who work out of the spotlight. Cyril Johnson was Ticket Secretary, Treasurer and Prompter for many years. They now hire their scenery but Eddie Ratcliffe is still their Scenic Designer. Although an independent group, they still use the name and still rehearse at the Folkhouse and their panto's, updated and rewritten, are based on previous productions.

'With music, comedy, song, dance and audience participation, there is something for all ages to enjoy in this traditional family pantomime'– this was the promise made in the 2009 reprise of 'Cinderella', and demonstrates how the original aim of the Westfield Folkhouse group has been faithfully maintained over the seventy years since their formation. It also indicates why they are still able to attract audiences from far and wide and how, after over forty years at the local Theatre, they are still playing to full houses.

Edward Taylor, John Dove and the Sherwood Dramatic Society

Edward Taylor began to write and direct plays while he was still at school. During the early part of W.W.II he organised and directed amateur plays and concerts for charity. Towards the end of the war, and holding the rank of Staff Sergeant, he was posted to the War Office in London. He joined the War Office Players where, after appearing in several productions, he took the leading role in R. C. Sherriff's 'Journey's End'.

While on 'demob' leave he took dancing lessons at Gladys Thorpe's Dancing School and it was at her invitation he joined the Mansfield Operatic Society. His first appearance with them was in 'Showboat' (1950) and he remained a member for the next fifteen years – singing, dancing and acting.

In 1961, encouraged by several well-known local actors, including Ron Hallam, Brian Stafford and Glenys Greaves, Ted founded his own amateur group, the Sherwood Amateur Dramatic Society, later to become the Sherwood Dramatic Society. From then on he was responsible for staging fifty productions at the local Theatre. These offered the whole range of theatrical experiences from humour to high drama. 'Never Too Late', one of their earlier plays, was a Midland Amateur Première and the 1974 production of 'Soft or a Girl', a rock musical, had the distinction of being the British Amateur Première.

To mark the twenty-fifth anniversary of their group they presented Terence Rattigan's 'The Winslow Boy'.

The Sherwood Dramatic Society
(IN ASSOCIATION WITH MANSFIELD DISTRICT COUNCIL)

present

THEIR 25th ANNIVERSARY PRODUCTION

THE WINSLOW BOY

by Terence Rattigan

✳ ✳ ✳

CIVIC THEATRE, MANSFIELD

12th - 16th February, 1985
at 7.15 p.m.

PROGRAMME

One of the most resounding successes of the Sherwood Dramatic Society came in September 1986 when they staged the British Amateur Première of 'Me Mam Sez' by local playwright, Barry Heath. This was directed by John Dove. The audience, over the eleven performances, exceeded five thousand. By popular demand, a further production of the play was presented in February 1987.

Action

The Scene is set in a typical Miner's terraced house in Mansfield at around 1942

Cast List

Jimmy	MICK CLIFTON
Mam	LINDA TURNER
Dennis	MALCOM BARNES
Doreen	SHAUNA MILNE
Doug	SIMON JONES
Sybil	JANE GORNOWICZ
Dad	JOHN DOVE
Maisie	NICOLA ELLIS
Jack	ANDREW DENNIS
Les	CHRIS STUBBS

Cast List 'Me Mam Sez' – 1987

Later that year, over six thousand people turned up at the Civic to see Barry's next play, 'Ya Shunta Joined' and, continuing their policy of promoting local talent, they staged Ann Hill's hilarious hospital comedy 'What You In For Duck?' before a large audience in October 1987 and before an even larger audience in 1988.

After twenty-five years as Director of Productions, Ted retired and became President of the Sherwood Dramatic Society. During his long career on the local amateur scene he also worked with the Penson Players and Masque Players. Although now completely retired from both acting and producing, Ted still maintains an interest in the Theatre as a member of the audience.

John Dove's first appearances on the Civic stage were in 1956/7 when at the ages of six and seven years old, he won first prizes for solo singing. In 1962, he took the stage again in Ralph Reader's 'Scout Gang Show' which featured local Scout groups, assisted by Cubs, Guides, Brownies and Rangers. The rousing opening of the traditional Gang Show song, 'Riding Along on the Crest of a Wave' was followed by a series of sketches. After this John took part in school plays, and later joined the Sutton Amateur Dramatic Society, for he was truly bitten by the acting bug.

In 1969, he was 'poached' from the Sutton group to make his debut with the Sherwood

Dramatic Society in 'Love on the Dole'. Such was his success with the group that, in 1975, he was a joint winner of the Harry Penson Golden Rose Bowl, presented by NANDA, for the best actor. This was for his part as 'Mick' in 'Soft or a Girl'.

Also a member of the Masque Productions and the Mansfield Operatic Society, John continued to be be an active and valuable member of the Sherwood Dramatic Society's team.

When Ted retired in 1980, he handed over to John who carried the group on to further successes, under its new name the Sherwood Theatre Company.

In 1990, John directed the third of Barry Heath's plays, 'Seaside Or Bust'. Brian Stafford, Linda Sindall, Ian Lee, Phil Bottomore and Jane Gornowicz all recreated the characters they had played in the first Barry Heath productions. When 'Me Mam Sez' was reprised in April 1994, Linda again played 'Mam' and Jane Gornowicz again played 'Sybil'. John took the part of 'Dad', as he did in the 1995 production of 'Ya Shunta Joined'. 'Soft or a Girl' was re-staged in 2001 and this proved to be their last production.

It was felt that a combination of the ever-rising costs of staging a production, the decline in audience numbers due to increased competition from films, T.V. and D.V.D's, plus the change of direction by the District Council to regional and professional theatre status led to the final curtain for the Sherwood Dramatic Society.

The Phoenix Theatre Group

Proceeds of the Phoenix Theatre Group shows were donated to a charitable organisation connected with the mining industry.

Eric Baker, Manager of Sherwood Colliery and Chairman of the players, writing in their Silver Jubilee presentation of 'The Sound of Music', said '. . . when our group was founded, the motives were a hobby, a form of self-expression, a demonstration of talents, usually frustrated in everyday life and a means of disseminating pleasure to a wide spectrum of people.'

Over the years they pursued these motives by presenting many well-loved musicals at the Civic, starting with 'Pyjama Game' and following that with 'Wedding in Paris'. In this, the scenery and costumes were designed and manufactured by the cast.

'Sweet Charity' (1970), 'Mame' (1972), 'Gigi' (1978) which also featured the Clipstone Colliery Welfare Band, and 'Irene' (1979), in which Kathryn Tyers played the title role, were all Nottinghamshire Premières.

Many actors, familiar in local music and drama circles often appeared with the Pheonix Theatre Group. Included in the cast of 'Call Me Madam' (1965) was Ron Hallam, who stepped into the part of Henry Gibson, at the last moment. He was also in 'Annie Get Your Gun' (1966) and in charge of make-up in 'Waltz Time'(1967), which his brother, Maurice produced. Brian Stafford, took part in 'Finian's Rainbow' (1969) and 'Mame' (1972).

In 'Gigi', the sets were designed, constructed and painted by Peter Thistlethwaite. Peter also played 'Edward Moulton Barrett' in 'Robert and Elizabeth'. In 'The King and I' (1975), he was in the cast and he also painted the sets.

On numerous occasions, Roger Brown appeared on stage, worked as Assistant Stage Manager, helped in painting sets and was in charge of publicity.

Josè Cooke took part in 'Fings Ain't What They Used To Be' (1978) and her daughter, Lisa, often featured as a dancer in musicals such as 'Gigi' and 'The King and I'.

Ken Cox, for many years a member of the Penson Players and also the Mansfield Operatic Society (he directed their Centenary Concert in 2007), was also responsible for many of the Pheonix Players productions.

Two of the founder members, Pat Grimly, Ticket Secretary, and Betty Teanby, Producer and Choreographer, who had remained active members of the Pheonix Theatre Group up to its Silver Jubilee were still with them when, celebrating their fortieth anniversary, they disbanded owing to ever-increasing costs. Pat carried on in amateur dramatics and is still a member of the Skegby Parish Players. Betty keeps very active in theatrical circles, especially with the Retford Operatic Society. She is also on the Rotary Club 'Junior Showtime' panel.

The name of the group is kept alive with the Pheonix Players' Bursary, awarded for the most promising performance in the Drama section of the Mansfield Music and Drama Festival.

As well as bringing popular entertainment to the people of Mansfield these, and all other non-professional users of the Civic Hall, were responsible for their own advertising, ticket selling and staffing of the Theatre, both backstage and front of house. Their continued enthusiasm and pride in their work helped, in no small measure, to bridge the gaps which were still being left by Council sponsored events and other entities who occasionally hired the premises.

An example of this was in November 1964, when the Nottingham and Nottinghamshire Drama Association and the British Drama League, as part of the Shakespeare Quatercentenary Celebration, jointly presented 'The Comedy of Errors' at the Civic. The souvenir programme noted that the production had received a great deal of assistance from (among others) Leslie Orton and Gunners China Store (Proprietor - P. Thistletwaite).

The Mansfield and District Youth Committee also made good use of the Theatre.

John Irons

As part of the Mansfield and District Youth Week, John Irons wrote and produced three farcical revues, 'Mansfield Ails' (1966), 'Mansfield Ails Again' (1967) and 'Somewhere Over the Slagheap' (1970) which were all staged at the Civic Hall and were reported to be 'fast, slick and well-received by an audience who obviously enjoyed seeing local personalities and events lampooned'. At this time, John was running the Youth Fellowship at St. Mark's Church and its members provided the core of the cast, although youngsters from the Mansfield area were also invited to participate. In July 1968 the Mansfield Youth Theatre was formed in order to provide young amateurs with an opportunity to gain experience in all aspects of the theatre, while working with their contemporaries. The average age of the players was seventeen and they were drawn from local youth groups. John was a member of the Mansfield and District Youth Committee which sponsored the venture and in September of that year, with Betty Teanby as Choreographer and Margaret Kirk as Musical Director, John produced 'Salad Days'. A young soprano, Ann Wilson, (the future Mrs. Irons) successfully auditioned for the leading role. After finishing her studies, Ann joined 'Cantamus' as a Teacher and is now Principal of the Training Choir. John accompanies 'Cantamus' on their travels, far and wide, to give a helping hand and solve any problems which may crop up along the way. John's interest in amateur dramatics began at High Oakham School, when he helped out his teacher, T. G. Martin, in school plays. When Tom Martin went on to form the Forest Players, John became part of the group and acted in several of their productions. One of the early members of the Sherwood Dramatic Society, his first part was in their 1971 production of 'When We Are Married'. He later appeared in 'A Man For All Seasons', a play which he had previously produced at St. Mark's. In 1981 he joined the Penson Players in 'Hindle Wakes'. After complimenting the actors, Ronald Parr, Theatre Critic, added, **'Finally a word of tribute to the audience who not only packed the Civic Theatre throughout the week's run but, by their warm and sympathetic response, contributed so richly to the unmistakable and exciting aura of theatrical success.'** In 1982 John began to work full-time for the Boys' Brigade. Being based in Nottingham and with commitments all over the county he had to give up his dramatic work in Mansfield, although his interest still remained. Now retired, he is still 'does bits and pieces, here and there' mainly acting in sketches on social occasions at St. Mark's and for the Boys' Brigade.

Originally, the General Purposes Committee of the Borough Council had been entrusted with all matters concerning the Civic Hall. Later this task passed to the Markets and Civil Building Committee but, in May 1966, it was resolved to transfer the responsibility for the repair, maintenance and control of the Theatre to the Library and Museum Committee whose members began to take steps, sometimes controversial, to improve existing conditions and widen the scope of programmes being offered to the public.

At one of their first meetings, it was decided that a 'Forthcoming Attraction' board should be displayed at the Theatre and that box office facilities should be provided, on a part-time

46

basis, for the benefit of societies using the Hall and for the convenience of the public. It was also resolved that all hirers of the Hall be required to use this service, for which a commission of 5% on all tickets sold should be charged. The Committee also let it be known they were anxious to provide entertainment of a more 'cultured' nature than that which was currently being staged.

Through its 'Our View' column and commenting on a meeting on September 1966, the Chad stated, **'It looks as though the Mansfield Council have decided it is time we were 'cultured'. For they are considering having an expert to guide them on Council sponsored events at the Civic Hall in order to regulate the choice of artistes and companies to ensure a more balanced programme … We don't believe it is the duty of the Council to provide for a cultured education in the positive manner which is implied by the Theatre. Cultural opportunities provided by a library service and art gallery are one thing. But the Theatre is much less adapted to catering for minority interests and in our view a civic theatre should cater for a catholicity of tastes having regard to the box office receipts as an indication of preference, if not profit.'**

In line with their intent to offer a more balanced perspective of the arts, even if it did reflect the tastes of the minority, the Library and Museum Committee had already authorised Councillor Max Banks, who had been elected to the Council in 1964, to attend a meeting of the recently formed National Council for Civic Theatres (N.C.T.T.). Mansfield, along with eighty-seven other Councils, became a member. Councillor Banks was elected to its Executive Committee which came to a Civic Reception in the Mayor's Parlour at the Town Hall in November 1966 and were entertained to lunch at the Civic Hall. Mr. Birks, General Secretary of the N.C.C.T., said the meeting at Mansfield was to discuss the first of their professional theatre tours which was to start early in 1967. 'The provinces have been denied the opportunity of getting first-class theatre touring companies. We hope to rectify this,' he said.

One consequence of this meeting came early in 1967, when the Committee recommended that, as from the following January, the hiring of the Hall for rehearsals should be restricted to one day prior to the first public performance. This news prompted a strong reaction from the ten local groups who frequently used the Theatre. The Borough Council, however, decided not to accept the Committee's recommendation. Instead, it called a meeting of the regular users to discuss the ways in which the time the Hall was available for public performances could be increased.

Councillor Banks explained that the recommendation had arisen from his reporting that the N.C.C.T. had offered the town a production which it was sending on tour, only to find that the weeks it was available were booked up by rehearsals. This was the type of problem which faced the Committee when considering putting on their own productions. Bookings which covered the seven months between August 1966 and April 1967 revealed that over eleven weeks had been devoted to rehearsals, which could have taken place elsewhere. This situation made it difficult for the Committee to organise their own programmes.

A case in point was that the proposed Mansfield Festival, was having to be held, not on a week which the Committee would have chosen, but on a week that the Civic Hall was available.

Mansfield Festival

Early in 1966 the Council, following a suggestion put to it by the Civic Hall Committee, had decided it would sponsor a festival in the following year. A Festival Committee was formed and according to an enthusiastic article in the Chad, 'Every effort was made to see that this was as fully representative as possible and that every shade of opinion was on it - experts, laymen, egg-heads, and the common people.' The Chairman of this Committee was Councillor Max Banks; a post he was to occupy for many years.

The first Mansfield Festival week made its bow in March 1967 when, according the Chad, the results of the Committee's hard work would be exposed to the public's critical view.

In addition to the events at the Civic, a Festival Ball, with Cyril Stapleton and his Orchestra and a Festival Beat Dance were held at the Palais de Danse. There were also lunch-time recitals at St. Peter's Church.

On the whole, the letters printed in the next edition of the Chad were positive. One correspondent was of the view that the organisers had done an excellent job in covering the arts and were to be congratulated on the high standard achieved but it was hoped they would not be deterred from future efforts by small capacity audiences.

Chad, March 2ⁿᵈ 1967

Owing to a government request that all expenditure should be cut the Council had decided, in January 1968, that there would be no Mansfield Festival in 1969. One councillor felt that, if the Festival had been a success in 1968 it would not have been cut out at this time. Another councillor, while deploring the move, said 'The money at stake is probably equivalent to a half penny rate - we are talking about £1,000'.

Fortunately, the Policy Committee was persuaded to reverse this decision and, by January 1969, the dates of the second Mansfield Festival had already been announced. It took place in October and offered a varied programme which ranged from Acker Bilk and his Paramount Jazz Band to the Royal Ballet. The Stockport Youth Orchestra was presented by the Mansfield and District Music Club and there was also a concert given by the newly-formed Festival Chorus.

Over the years, the Mansfield Festival became an exciting annual event but it was not always free from controversy.

Speaking in 1971, at the inaugural service at St. Peter's Church, the Archdeacon of Chesterfield said, 'There may have been some criticism about the expenditure of public money on holding a Festival, despite there being many other urgent and necessary schemes needing money - more parking spaces, new street lighting, additional clinics, but people have more spiritual needs. It was not enough that a town should be administratively efficient. The Council's chief concern should be with the spirit of its people and the quality of their life'. The service was conducted by the Rural Dean, the Reverend R. T. Warburton. The lesson was read by the Chairman of the Festival Committee, Councillor M. Banks. The organist and choirmaster was Mr. M. Cousins.

This particular Festival fortnight got off to a flying start with a concert organised by the Mansfield Folk Club which, as reported in the CHAD 'had the audience stomping, clapping and singing along'. On Sunday, the audience had a wonderful evening's entertainment from the Band of the Royal Marines. Kenny Ball and his Jazzmen appeared on the Monday evening and 'gave a performance of rip-roaring razzmatazz, that gave to traditional jazz and the modern ballad the family atmosphere which suited the capacity audience'.

The Festival continued with what was to become an almost traditional event - the concert put on by the winners from the Music Festival in June. The soloists were accompanied by Walter Hepple, David Chamberlain and Michael Neaum. The show was organised and introduced by Mr. A. Steele, Deputy Director of the Mansfield Education Committee.

During the second week there was also a concert by the Sheffield Symphony Orchestra 'which confessed to being pleased to play at Mansfield before a capacity audience'. At a performance of Rossini's 'Barber of Seville' 'a large audience took refuge from a wet and miserable English evening to be transformed to the warmth and gaiety of sunny Spain'.

The Mansfield Festival was continuing to add to the Civic's reputation as a hub of activity for entertainment, culture and public amenities.

Among the 1983 attractions were Humphrey Lyttleton and his band, the Johnny Morris Family Show, a live broadcast of the popular B.B.C. Radio Programme 'Any Questions', with David Jacobs in the chair, the Allegri String Quartet and Moira Anderson.

As they had done since 1976, young musicians from Heiligenhaus took part in the Festival. In 1976 and 1978 the Accordion Orchestra gave concerts. In 1978, 1983 and 1991 the Youth Symphony Orchestra appeared on the Civic stage.

Max Banks, who had been largely instrumental in guiding the formation of the Festival and in enhancing and expanding its activities, resigned as Chairman of the Mansfield and District Arts Association in 1992.

CIVIC THEATRE

LEEMING STREET, MANSFIELD.
Box Office: 22561–296
23882 Eve. & Weekend

SATURDAY 10th SEPTEMBER 1983   at 7.30 p.m.
Warsop & District Organ Society present
MARK SHAKESPEARE IN CONCERT
Adults £1.50   Children/ OAP £1.00

SUNDAY 11th SEPTEMBER, 1983   at 7.30 p.m.
Supporters of the Samaritans present a Brass Band Concert
Featuring THE SHIRLAND BAND
Adults £1.50   Children/OAP £1.00

FRIDAY 16th SEPTEMBER, 1983   at 7.30 p.m.
ROBERT YOUNG
'The Golden Voice of Europe'
Adults £2.50   Children/OAP £2.00

SATURDAY 17th SEPTEMBER, 1983   at 5.30 p.m.
GOSPEL HIGHLIGHTS
Adults £2.00   Children/OAP £1.50

WEDNESDAY 21st SEPTEMBER, 1983   at 7.30 p.m.
Mansfield District Council Leisure Services present:—
LONNIE DONEGAN
Plus supporting acts.
Adults £3.00   Children/OAP £2.50

TUESDAY 27th SEPTEMBER to
SATURDAY 1st OCTOBER, 1983   at 7.30 p.m.
Sherwood Dramatic Society present:—
ABIGAILS PARTY
A modern comedy by Mike Leight
Adults £1.25   Children/OAP £1.00
(Reductions for Party bookings)

* *

THURSDAY 6th OCTOBER to

SUNDAY 23rd OCTOBER, 1983

MANSFIELD FESTIVAL

WATCH PRESS FOR DETAILS

* *

SUNDAY 16th OCTOBER, 1983   at 7.00 p.m.
Mansfield District Council Leisure Services presents
(as part of Mansfield Festival)
C.W.S. (MANCHESTER) BRASS BAND
Adults £1.60   Children/OAP £1.00

FRIDAY 21st OCTOBER, 1983   at 6.30 p.m. and 9.00 p.m.
Mansfield District Council Leisure Services presents:—
(as part of Mansfield Festival)
THE FABULOUS FLYING PICKETS
Adults £3.00   Children/OAP £2.00

MONDAY 24th OCTOBER. 1983   at 7.30 p.m.
ANTOINETTE THEATRE DANCE SCHOOL
Annual Display
Adults £1.50   Children 75p

TUESDAY 25th OCTOBER, 1983   at 7.30 p.m.
Meet the ROYAL SOCIETY for the PROTECTION OF BIRDS
including R.S.P.B. film and illustrated talk
Adults £1.25   Children/OAP 70p
Tickets available from Box Office from 26th September, 1983

MONDAY 31st OCTOBER to
SATURDAY 5th NOVEMBER, 1983   at 7.15 p.m.
Masque Productions present:—
'HELLO DOLLY'
Adults £2.00/£1.50   Children/OAP £1.50/£1.00
(Reductions for Party Bookings)

MONDAY 7th NOVEMBER to
SATURDAY 12th NOVEMBER, 1983 at 7.30 p.m.
Penson Players present:—
'FRINGE BENEFITS'
Monday Front Stalls 70p Rear Stalls 60p
Tuesday to Saturday: Front Stalls £1.00 Rear Stalls 80p

SUNDAY 13th NOVEMBER, 1983   at 7.00 p.m.
Mansfield District Council Leisure Services present:—
THE FAIREY ENGINEERING BRASS BAND
Adults £1.60   Children/OAP £1.00

SUNDAY 20th NOVEMBER at   7.30 p.m.
Multiple Sclerosis Charity Show
'IT'S COUNTRY'
Starring Misty Mountain, Gretts Outlaws, Roy Clarke
PLUS SPECIAL GUEST ARTIST
Compere Ken Puffer
Adults £1.50   Children/OAP 75p

TUESDAY 22nd NOVEMBER, 1983 at 7.30 p.m.
BRITISH MEAT COOKERY DEMONSTRATION
Details from the Box Office

MONDAY 28th NOVEMBER to
SATURDAY 3rd DECEMBER, 1983 at 7.30 p.m.
Phoenix Theatre Group present:—
'THE KING AND I'
Adults £1.75   Children/OAP £1.25
(Monday all seats £1.25)

SUNDAY 4th DECEMBER, 1983   at 7.30 p.m.
Mansfield District Council Leisure services present:—
"THE BLACK ABBOTTS CHRISTMAS SPECIAL"
Adults £3.50   Children/OAP £2.50

MONDAY, 5th DECEMBER to
SATURDAY 10th DECEMBER, 1983
Mansfield District Council Leisure Services in conjunction
with Barrie Stacey Productions present:—
TALES FROM HANS CHRISTIAN ANDERSEN
Monday to Friday 10.00 a.m. and 2.00 p.m.
Saturday 2.00 p.m. and 6.00 p.m.
Adults £1.50   Children/OAP 80p

WEDNESDAY 7th DECEMBER, 1983   at 7.30 p.m.
Eminent Organ Demonstration by
JOHN MANN
Tickets available from the Mansfield Organ Centre Leeming St.

FRIDAY 9th DECEMBER, 1983   at 7.30 p.m.
Mansfield District Council Leisure Services present:—
BLASTER BATES
Adults: Centre Stalls £3.00   Side Stalls and Circle £2.50
Children/OAP All seats £2.00

MONDAY 12th to SATURDAY 17th DECEMBER, 1983
Mansfield District Council Leisure Services present:—
"THE HOUSE THAT SOOTY BUILT"
Monday and Tuesday 5.00 p.m.
Wednesday, Thursday, and Friday 2.15 p.m and 5.15 p.m.
Saturday 11.00 a.m. and 2.30 p.m.
All seats £1.60

WEDNESDAY 21st DECEMBER, 1983 at 7.30 p.m.
CHRISTMAS WITH CANTAMUS
Adults £2.00   Children/OAP £1.50

SATURDAY 7th to SATURDAY 14th JANUARY, 1984
Westfield Folk House presents:—
"DICK WHITTINGTON"
Monday to Friday 7.15 p.m. Saturday 2.30 p.m. and 7.15 p.m.
Sunday 6.15 p.m.

Max Banks flanked by Michael Foot and local MP Alan Meale

This was the year the Festival celebrated its twenty-fifth anniversary, with a return of the Vienna Festival Ballet performing 'Sleeping Beauty', the Temperance Seven Jazz Band, Johnny Ball's 'Think of a Number', based on his award-winning television series and Bob Geldof.

The Mansfield Festival continued until 1997, when it became increasingly expensive to include the top-name artists who had become such a feature over the preceding years. The Council reviewed its arts policy and decided that any future festivals should be more community based.

Bearing this policy in mind, the Festival was revived in 2008 and was dedicated to the memory of Max Banks, a life long supporter of art and culture in Mansfield.

MANSFIELD ARTS FESTIVAL
"At a Glance"

DATE	TIME	PERFORMANCE	VENUE
Friday 2nd October	8.00pm	Joe Loss Orchestra	Mansfield Leisure Centre
Sunday 4th October &			
Monday 5th October &			
Tuesday 6th October	7.30pm	Vienna Festival Ballet	Mansfield Civic Theatre
Wednesday 7th October	8.00pm	Bob Geldof	Mansfield Civic Theatre
Thursday 8th October	7.00pm	Mansfield Lions Club	Mansfield Civic Theatre
Saturday 10th October	7.15pm	Rock Showcase	Mansfield Leisure Centre
Saturday 10th October	7.30pm	Mick Smith and Friends	Mansfield Civic Theatre
Sunday 11th October	7.30pm	Caliche	Mansfield Civic Theatre
Sunday 11th October	7.30pm	Mansfield Choral Society with The Mansfield Handel Orchestra	Mansfield Leisure Centre
Monday 12th October	10am & 1pm	Disabled Day of Dance	Mansfield Arts Centre
Monday 12th October	7.30pm	East of England Orchestra String Trio	Mansfield Arts Centre
Tuesday 13th October	10am & 2pm	Johnny Ball's - "Think of a Number"	Mansfield Civic Theatre
Tuesday 13th October	7.30pm	Trestle Theatre Company – "Hanging Around"	Mansfield Arts Centre
Wednesday 14th October to Saturday 17th October	7.30pm	The Penson Players	Mansfield Civic Theatre
Thursday 15th October	7.30pm	Stage One Company	Mansfield Arts Centre
Friday 16th October	1.00pm	"Lunchtime Lilt" Concert	Mansfield Arts Centre
Friday 16th October	3.00pm	Bill Varnam "Soup, Soap and Salvation"	Mansfield Arts Centre
Friday 16th October	7.30pm	Rachel Sherry: Harpist & Soprano	Tudor Barn: Warsop Parish Centre
Saturday 17th October	7.30pm	The Kala Chethena Kathakali Troupe	Mansfield Arts Centre
Sunday 18th October	2.30pm	Music and Drama - Winners	Mansfield Civic Theatre
Sunday 18th October	2.45pm 3.15pm	Organ Recital and Choral EvenSong	St Peters and St Pauls Church
Monday 19th October	7.30pm	Temperance Seven	Mansfield Civic Theatre
Tuesday 20th October	7.30pm	London Arts Trio	Mansfield Arts Centre
Tuesday 20th October	7.30pm	Mansfield Male Voice Choir and Heiligenhaus Frohsinn 1867EV	Mansfield Civic Theatre
Wednesday 21st October	7.45pm	Please Y'self	Mansfield Civic Theatre
Thursday 22nd October to Saturday 24th October	7.30pm	Mansfield Community Opera	Mansfield Leisure Centre
Thursday 22nd October	10.30am & 1.30pm	Playtime Percussion Roadshow	Mansfield Civic Theatre
Thursday 22nd October	7.30pm	"Walk Right Back" (To the sounds of the Everly Brothers)	Mansfield Civic Theatre
Friday 23rd October	2.00pm	Linda Darnell	Mansfield Arts Centre
Thursday 29th October	1.30pm	Neales Antiques Roadshow	Mansfield Art Gallery
Friday 30th October	8.00pm	The Phantom is Back/ Dave Willetts	Mansfield Leisure Centre
Sunday 1st November	11.30am - 5.30pm 7 - 10pm	Asian Arts & Cultural Festival	Mansfield Civic Centre

From Mansfield Arts Festival 25th Anniversary Programme, 1992

51

Both before, and after, the Library and Museum Committee took over the responsibility for the Civic Hall, the pattern of annual productions, established in the early days, continued to flourish. The Theatre was also occasionally hired out to private organisations:-

Chad, January 19th 1967

The Corporation also sponsored their own events. Among these were brass band concerts (Ransome and Marles, Foden's Motors), and orchestral concerts (the New Sheffield Symphony Orchestra and the Midland Sinfonia Orchestra, with Leon Goosens as soloist). They also presented the Derby Playhouse Company in three performances of 'The Promise', a serious dramatic play by Alexei Arbuznov, which starred Tamara Ustinov.

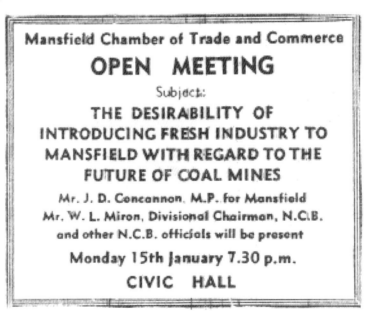

Chad, January 11th 1968

In a lighter vein, the Chesterfield Operatic Society was engaged to give ten performances of 'Calamity Jane', which was produced by Leslie Orton.

One of the Corporation's proudest achievements was in January 1968 when they sponsored John Ogdon's first piano recital at the Civic Hall.

John Ogdon (1937 - 1989)

It was Miss Nellie Houseley, John Ogdon's first piano teacher, who recognised and nurtured his outstanding talent. She was particularly impressed when he introduced himself as John 'Rachmaninov' Ogdon - it boded well for the future. John went on to study at the Manchester Royal College of Music and began his professional career when, standing in for another pianist, he amazed the audience with the virtuosity of his playing. In 1958, at the age of twenty-one he made his London debut at the 'Proms' and in 1961 was awarded the Liszt Prize in Budapest. At the age of twenty-five, he was declared the joint winner, with Vladimir Ashkenazy, of the prestigious International Tchaikovsky Competition in Moscow, which led to him being internationally acknowledged as one of the greatest pianists of the century. He possessed enormous technical resources, an amazing memory and incredible sight-reading skills which enabled him to prepare new pieces of extreme difficulty in the shortest possible time.

John Ogdon - Recital at the Civic, April 1983
Back Row: Richard Priest (Tenor), David Chamberlain (Conductor), Robert Turner (Bass).
Front Row: Jeanette Christian, John Ogdon, Pamela Cook MBE (Senior Tutor), Kym Cooper.

Ill-health dogged him throughout his career but did not diminish his genius. John, who was born in Mansfield Woodhouse, often returned to Mansfield, giving recitals in the theatre

53

Chad - October 1987

The President of the Mansfield Music and Drama Festival, Mrs. Sheila Haslam, making a presentation to John Ogdon on the occasion of the 50th birthday celebration concert in the Civic Theatre on October 16th 1987.

Commissioned Bust of John Ogdon

of the Chesterfield Road Technical College but, in January 1968, he appeared at the Civic Hall, in a concert arranged by the Mansfield and District Music Club and sponsored by the Borough Council. Here, before a capacity audience, as the Chad reported, 'he demonstrated the qualities which had earned him universal acclaim. It was an evening which will remain in the memories of those privileged to hear this great player.' On a return visit the Chad reported that 'The Mansfield Festival opened in a truly magnificent style when an enthusiastic audience were treated to an outstanding performance by virtuoso pianist, John Ogdon.' In April 1983, he performed Liszt's oratorio 'Christus' at the Civic, with the Mansfield Choral Society conducted by David Chamberlain and soloists from the Birmingham School of Music, coached by Pamela Cook, Senior Lecturer in the Vocal Studies Department.

John was welcomed back in October 1987 to participate, once more, in the Mansfield Festival, with a special concert to celebrate his fiftieth birthday. In July 1989, at London's Queen Elizabeth Hall and in what proved to be his last concert, he received a standing ovation. In August that year his brilliant career was tragically cut short when, at the age of fifty-two, he succumbed to pneumonia. Since his death, John's name has continued to be recognised and honoured by the local community. The 'John Ogdon Awards' which are given to outstanding classical music students aged fourteen to twenty-one years, are sponsored by Mansfield District Council.

The late John Wakefield, known to all as Jack, one of John Ogdon's most ardent admirers, raised funds to commission a sculpture from the artist Joy Bently, which was unveiled in the foyer of the Palace Theatre on April 13th 2002, by the Chairman of Mansfield District Council, Councillor Malcolm Sage.

Andrew Tucker, Hilary Ward, John Wakefield.

55

Ben Nolan is a professional tuner of great repute who maintained the Theatre's old Bechstein piano for many years, even storing it in his parents' house during the refurbishment. Ben lives in Southwell and has not lost contact with the venerable Bechstein, for it is now located in the Great Hall of the Bishop's Palace.

Picture courtesy of Ben Nolan
Ben Nolan (centre) with his brother and sister, seated at the Theatre's Bechstein in 1968.

When it was deemed that a new grand piano was urgently needed, local musician, Hilary Ward, an enthusiastic supporter of live music in the town, set herself the task of raising the considerable sum of money needed to buy this replacement. Among the many people who were willing to answer her appeal, it was particularly gratifying for Hilary to receive a generous donation from Vladimir Ashkenazy. Purchased on the recommendation of Ben Nolan, a superb Yamaha C7 was received on June 6th 2004 at the Theatre, on behalf of the people of Mansfield, by the Vice-Chairman of the District Council, Councillor Norman Cook. Pianist Sam Hayward, then treated his audience to a special inaugural performance on the 'John Ogdon Grand Piano'.

The Palace Music Society hold an annual piano recital to celebrate the birthday (January 27th) of this truly great and talented musician.

Mansfield & District Male Voice Choir

On Sunday 25th February 1968 the Corporation presented the Mansfield and District Male Voice Choir in a Sunday afternoon celebrity concert; the guest artistes were the principal soprano and tenor from the Sadler's Wells Opera Company. Conducted by their Musical Director, Harry Smith, the choir, in the opinion of the Chad, 'showed again the ability which has made it such a first-rate group'.

Harry Smith had achieved national fame in the 1940's when the High Oakham School Choir, where he was then teaching music, made several radio appearances on the 'Black and White Minstrel Show'. He was Musical Director of the Male Voice Choir for twenty-five years. It was at another Civic Celebrity Concert in 1968 that he made his final appearance. He was later awarded an O.B.E. for his services to music.

Walter Pitchford was eighteen when he joined the Choir and was with them in 1968, when they moved from the Grand to the Civic Hall. Allowing for the several years he had to take off owing to ill health, he has been a member for forty-eight years and is now Chairman. Although he still sings, Walter has recently decided to give up solo work. Their Celebrity Concerts, both at the Grand and the Civic, featured top-class artistes, including the Max Jaffa Trio, Campoli, the violinist and singers such as John Hanson, Joan Hammond, John Heddle Nash and Owen Brannigan. Walter regrets that, at today's prices, the Choir cannot afford to invite present-day celebrities to join them.

Nevertheless, over the years, the Choir has continued to attract large audiences at the local Theatre, to gain wider acclaim and further accolades.

When they won the Cheltenham Musical Festival Gold Cup for the second time they returned home to a Civic Reception. On this occasion they were presented with the coat of arms of Mansfield and given permission to use it as a badge on their jackets.

They exchange visits with the Frohsinn Male Voice Choir of Mansfield's twin-town, Heiligenhaus, and have sung with them at the Palace.

From the Mansfield Arts Festival 25th Anniversary Programme, 1992.

They also take part in the British Legion's Festival of Remembrance and have done so since it was first held at the Theatre. In March 2009, with their current Musical Director, Meryl Chambers, they gave a Concert Preview of their forthcoming contribution to the '1,000 Voices Concert' at the Royal Albert Hall, London, which was organised by the Welsh Association of Male Voice Choirs. Of the twenty-five groups taking part they had the honour of being one of the only two who were English. With fifty-three members paying an annual subscription, the Mansfield Male Voice Choir is largely self-financed.

They travel to many parts of the country, as well as being much in demand in Mansfield and surrounding district. Chairman Walter reports that their diary is full of engagements and that he and his fellow-choristers are looking forward to continuing bringing pleasure to their audiences well into the future.

With these continuing efforts to widen the scope of programmes presented and to ensure the premises were used to a greater extent, the Committee felt much more needed to be done. Some members were of the opinion that the name 'CIVIC HALL' gave the wrong idea of its true purpose; that the general public and people outside the town had the impression it was only used for 'civic' purposes such as meetings.

A new name was chosen and a new era was about to begin.

PART FIVE

THE CIVIC THEATRE
1969 – 1995

The official name-change came in January 1969. No longer a 'Hall', the 'Theatre' continued to be generally referred to as 'The Civic'.

Chad, January 2ⁿᵈ 1969

This was just one of the concerts cited in the 'Letters to the Editor' column of the Chad (23ʳᵈ January 1969).

It was the writer's opinion that 'The Mansfield Corporation deserves a large bouquet for the various musical enterprises of the last few months. Many more of these and the Civic will earn the accolade of the 'Music Mecca of the Midlands'.

The Corporation continued, with varying success, to sponsor 'musical enterprises'. In February, the Royal Ballet presented 'Ballet for All' - in the programme it was noted that 'because of the small stage at the Civic, there will be no corps de ballet'. In March the Mansfield and District Music Club offered Donizetti's comic opera 'L'Elisir d'Amore', staged in costume and sung in English. According to the Chad Theatre Critic, 'The elegant and entertaining production delighting both the eye and the ear did not deserve to be faced with empty seats'.

Empty seats were never a problem for the Clipstone Sherwood Players. Founded by Harvey Coupe in the 1940's, they made their début at the Civic in 1959 with a four-day run of 'Reluctant Heroes'. Linda Turner (née Coupe) remembers the immense pride she felt at the success of her father's first venture on to the larger stage of the Civic. She also remembers the spooky experience of being accidentally locked in an underground dressing room during the aptly-named 1966 production of 'Wanted One Body'.

Clipstone Sherwood Players
have
"SOMETHING TO HIDE"
(by Leslie Sands)

BOOK NOW at the
CIVIC THEATRE
to find out what it is
March 5th—8th
Seats 3/6 and 4/6 (OAP 2/0
2/6)

Printed this way at Advertiser's
request

Chad, February 27th 1969

Every year, for more than a decade, the Players steadily added to their initial success by entertaining their audiences with a variety of popular plays.

One of their last productions was 'Something to Hide'. From her early years of working with her father, Linda went on to appear many more times on the stage of the Civic and to make a valuable contribution to local amateur dramatics.

Other events which took place at this time were a Celebrity Concert by the Mansfield and District Male Voice Choir, which marked the last appearance of Harry Smith as Musical Director, and a concert featuring 'The Spinners', jointly presented by the Horse and Groom Folk Club and the West Nottinghamshire College Students' Association.

The Civic Theatre lounge was also put to use when the Mansfield and District Holidays for Fatherless Children Association held a well attended sherry and wine evening. The money raised was used to provide the children with a week's holiday in Norfolk.

In what was to become another traditional annual event, December 1969 saw the very first appearance in Mansfield of 'Sooty' and 'Sweep' - ably assisted by Harry Corbett.

The 'Sooty Show' was so eagerly anticipated by the younger generation of the town, that booking enquiries for the December performances began as early as May and year after year, the Theatre was filled to capacity.

Of the countless number of parents who have memories of the shows is Janet Roberts, who always took her daughter, now in her forties, to see 'Sooty'. At the time, Anna had severe speech problems and was virtually silent. The only time she became animated was at this show where in spite of Janet's best efforts, she kept running down the aisle. Although next day she was always hoarse, it briefly showed her true potential.

In 1978, Yvette Price Mear volunteered to work part time at the Civic. She became a Follow-Spot Operator and her greatest claim to fame was, when out of a blackout, she found 'Sooty' on the end of Matthew Corbett's hand. To do this, she had to open the follow-spot very carefully, in order to get a minuscule slither of light, so that when the curtains opened she was successfully on target.

The 'Sooty' spotlight also fell briefly on Margaret Shooter when she took her young son to see the show. John was invited to go on stage and help with a trick. He was eager to accept but not without his mother. Once they were both on stage John was too awestruck to perform, so Margaret had to stand in for him.

This was the first time Margaret had trodden the boards. Little did she imagine that, years later, she would appear in several Community Theatre productions on the same stage.

Doris Taylor, former Head of the Primary Department at Fountaindale Special School, has many happy memories of Harry and Matthew Corbett, who both forged strong links with the school.

When Harry appeared on the T.V. Show, 'This Is Your Life', the Principal of the school was one of the guests and brief shots of Fountaindale also featured in the programme.

Matthew, who took over Sooty when his father retired, maintained this close bond and always stayed at Fountaindale during the six days the show played at the Theatre. And, as in Harry's time, the whole Sooty team continued to give a special exclusive 'Fountaindale' performance for the students and staff, after their Christmas lunch.

Sooty, Sweep and Soo, now assisted by Matthew's successor Richard Cadell are still visiting Mansfield and still enchanting their many fans both old and new.

THE CANTAMUS GIRLS' CHOIR

Another long-term tradition was also established in the early years of the Civic Theatre. It was in December 1970, that the girls, then known as the Cantamus Ensemble, gave the first of their Christmas concerts at the Theatre.

Pamela Cook founded this small choir in order to help her individual pupils learn how to sing in a group. In their first year (1968), when they won the Berry Hill Musical Festival the adjudicator suggested the Ensemble entered international competitions. That this advice had been heeded was evident in the programme notes of 'Youth is a Pleasure', a programme of song and drama presented together with Unit Two of the Penson Players:

'The Cantamus Ensemble is to compete in the International Choral Festival in Montreux, Switzerland, in April, and your patronage is invited - minimum donation 50p. A tape recording of the choir and soloists will be sent to all who donate £2 or more'. The generous response to this appeal both surprised and was greatly appreciated by all concerned in organising this first trip abroad for, as reported in the Chad, 'The girls went out to Montreux unknown and came back celebrities' - having won second prize.

The girls were back at the Civic in July 1972, when they presented a joint recital with the Sophia Chamber Choir, an eminent Bulgarian ladies' choir. They returned in October to present a Slavonic Evening as part of the Mansfield Festival. This was also the year of the choir's first major prize when they entered the Bela Bartoc Contemporary Music Festival in Debrecen, Hungary.

**The programme, above, was one of the occasions when Cantamus made a
colourful contribution to the Mansfield Festival.**

At a Silver Jubilee Concert in July 1972, they took part in 'a Garland of British Harp Music Songs and Madrigals'. This was directed by Pamela Cook and the soloist was Osian Ellis, the Queen's harpist.

Since these early days, the Cantamus Girls' Choir has become world-famous, winning twenty-five first prizes in prestigious competitions at home and abroad.

Always under the directorship of their founder, who was awarded the MBE in 1984, the choir has sung with renowned orchestras, been featured in radio and television programmes, made CD's, DVD's and premièred works by celebrated composers.

Michael Neaum has become highly regarded for his arrangements which have been sung around the world. He retired in 2007, after three decades as accompanist to the choir.

Ann Irons and Elaine Guy (née Hazlewood), who are now vocal tutors, and the late Joy Nicol, all trained with Pamela Cook. Ann is also Director of the Junior Training Choir which was formed in 1992, taking girls from the age of nine.

When the choir celebrated its twenty-fifth anniversary in 1993, Sheila Haslam, who has been with Cantamus from the beginning, told a Chad reporter that she put down its success to Pamela Cook's teaching and the discipline she instils in the girls, whose ages in the main choir range from thirteen to nineteen.

In the opinion of Howard Goodall, composer, television presenter and Vice-President of the choir, 'Only very few musicians and performers manage to combine absolute world class excellence of technique and style with the ability to express themselves from the bottom of their hearts. Cantamus, miraculously, are among these select few'.

In the Chad 'Your View' column, 'Music Lover' wrote of the 1972 Christmas Concert '. . .that the choir really captured the Christmas Spirit, this being reflected in the rapturous applause of the capacity audience.' Written over thirty years ago, this sentiment still rings true. Not only at Christmas, 'rapturous applause' and 'capacity audiences' continue to mark every occasion when the stage of the Theatre is graced by the Cantamus Girls' Choir.

MASQUE PRODUCTIONS

AFFILIATED TO THE NATIONAL OPERATIC AND DRAMATIC ASSOCIATION
MASQUE PRODUCTIONS

When The Masque Players were disbanded in 1971, several former members decided to form a new company - Masque Productions. The original aim of the group was to offer a wide range of productions, encompassing plays (they made their Civic début with the drama 'Becket'), musicals and experimental drama. However, due in part to the preference of the general public for musicals, they had to narrow their scope and went on the follow the tradition established by the Masque Players.

Several familiar names appeared in the programme of their 1973 production of 'Camelot'. Among the cast were Peter Skinner and Michael Merry. Other credits were Ron Hallam (Director), Irene Morley (Choreography), Peter Skinner (Settings and Backcloths), Ian Hibbert (Musical Director) and Neil Butler (Lighting and Sound).

Neil, currently Chairman of Masque Productions, was one of the founder members. He had developed an interest in scenery, lighting and sound during his time with the Masque Players and he was able to use these skills.

In 'A Funny Thing Happened on the Way to the Forum' (1975), Neil helped with the construction and painting of the sets and was in charge of the lighting. He co-directed 'Sweet Charity' (1978) and then moved on to directing many of the group's major shows. One of his more recent productions was 'Oliver!', which he had first produced in 1982.

Joyce Buckingham, already well know for her many roles with the Sherwood Dramatic Society and the Mansfield Operatic Society, made her initial appearance in the 1982 'Oliver!' and soon became a regular and stalwart member of the team. In 1986 she took charge of 'Mini Masque' which introduced various branches of stagecraft to youngsters aged eight to fifteen. ('Mini Masque' later became 'The Junior Group' whose members are featured in as many productions as possible.)

Joyce, who is now an onlooker rather than a participant, modestly describes herself as 'an actress, who also happens to read music and sing' - this she claims, is the secret of her success on the amateur stage.

Linda Turner's first appearance with the Masque Productions was also in the 1982 'Oliver!' - in the chorus. The following year she was in 'Carousel', this time in a leading role. Like Joyce, Linda became a valued member of the group. She also served on the Committee and in 1987, with Sheryll Hardy, she co-directed and choreographed 'H.M.S. Pinafore'. Along with her other commitments to amateur dramatics, Linda directed and acted in several pantomimes at West Nottinghamshire College where she had, and still has, a 'day job'. Looking back, Linda marvels at how she coped with being a working mother of two young sons and still managed to find time for all her stage work.

Jill Benson is another much-esteemed and long serving member of Masque Productions. In spite of all her numerous other activities she has choreographed many of their musicals and also the two recent and successful variety shows.

These shows were conceived and directed by Geoff Fielden and Andrew Wolden, who have both appeared on-stage in many of the company's shows. In 2009, Andrew also stepped off-stage to produce 'Scrooge - the Musical'.

Once source of pride to members of Masque Productions, is the money they have raised over the last few years for their chosen charity 'Guide Dogs for the Blind'. The names of support dogs bought have usually been linked with a musical they have recently produced - Annie, Peter (Pan), Bugsy (Malone), and Benji (after the dog who played 'Toto' in the 'Wizard of Oz'). There was also 'Charlie', named in remembrance of an admirer who left a bequest to add to their donations.

The high standards of production and performance, maintained over their long association with the local Theatre, is another source of pride to members, past and present, of Masque Productions.

This appreciation of the Civic appeared in Chad's Midweek Extra (June 1979). **'It is now regarded as a 'little gem of a theatre' and while the seating capacity is slightly under five hundred, it has become the focal point in the town for the Musical Festival, three amateur operatic societies, numerous drama groups, talent competitions, professional musical and light entertainment concerts, pop concerts and other stage productions.**

It is also the centre of entertainment for Mansfield's annual festival in October, when big bands, pop groups, operatic companies and several 'top drawer' artistes are invited to appear at the Civic Theatre. Nearly 65,000 people paid to see shows there last year.

The foyer and the lounge also cater for more convivial occasions such as bring-and-buy sales and coffee mornings.

It was recently estimated that a further 15,000 people attended events of this nature last year. And this means that approximately 80,000 people visited the Civic for one reason or another.

The acoustic qualities are considered to be among the finest in the district and many performers have sung the praises, and spoken, of the pleasure they have received from

acting, dancing and singing on the stage.

A large part of the credit for this prestige can be claimed by Stage Manager, Mr. Colin Carter, who started work at the Civic more than six years ago'.

Colin Carter

Colin came to the Civic in the early 1970's but his theatrical career had begun much earlier when, at the age of fourteen, he became a part-time stage-hand at the former Grand Theatre. On leaving school, he took on full-time employment as a Projectionist/Follow Spotter, depending on whether a film or live show was on the programme.

He later took a course, organised by the National Association of Theatre and Kinema Employees, in Theatre and Kine Science and Technology, and came first among students from Nottinghamshire, Derbyshire and Leicestershire.

While serving in the R.A.F. during his National Service, he was able to broaden the scope of his experience. Stationed in Norfolk, and thanks to a former colleague from the Grand, who was now Manager of the Regal Theatre, Great Yarmouth, Colin came into contact with such stars as Vera Lynn, Max Bygraves and the Beverley Sisters.

On returning to Mansfield, he travelled round local theatres gaining more experience in stage management and lighting, until he was offered the post of Stage Manager at the Civic.

In 1982, by which time Colin had been promoted to Theatre Manager, the Theatre was closed for two months for refurbishment and improvement of facilities. New seats, a new public address system and a computerised lighting board were installed. The old changing

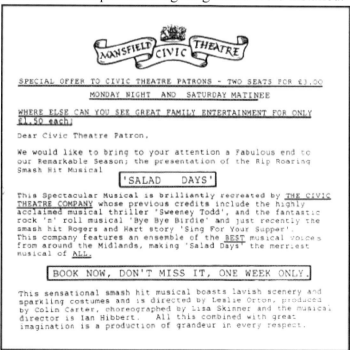

rooms under the stage were modified and new changing rooms replaced the old Pit Theatre, which had been an informal space created from disused buildings next to the theatre.

Under Colin's guidance, an attractive programme was arranged to mark the reopening of the 'New Look Civic'. Included on it were the Brighouse and Rastrick Band, the Pasadena Roof Orchestra, 'Operetta for All', with Angela Jenkins and John Noble, 'The Wizard of Oz' and 'Sooty's Circus.'

The Mansfield Festival was continuing to add to the Civic's reputation as a hub of activity for entertainment, culture and public amenities.

Among the 1983 attractions were Humphrey Lyttleton and his band, the Johnny Morris Family Show, a live broadcast of the popular B.B.C. Radio Programme 'Any Questions', with David Jacobs in the chair, the Allegri String Quartet and Moira Anderson.

In May 1988, Colin produced the musical 'Bugsy Malone', with a cast of forty-three local children. The overwhelming success of this and the eagerness of the cast to know what they were going to do next, led to the launching of the Civic Theatre School for Children. This opened in September and aimed to teach all aspects of theatre from acting, mime, dancing and singing to make-up, sound and lighting. The Tutors included Lisa Skinner, Chris Ponka, Jeannette Barns, Tamsyn Smith and former professional actress, Sylvia Jackson. Their first presentations were two revues 'Beginners Please' and 'Beginners Please -Take Two'. Among later productions were 'Smike' and 'Wiz'. After attending the Theatre School, several members went on to become professionally connected with the Theatre. Others went on to join the amateur dramatic companies which regularly used the Civic.

The formation of the Civic Theatre Company was another of Colin's innovations. The first in-house presentation was 'Crown Matrimonial' (1975) directed by Leslie Orton and produced by Colin. This was followed by a string of other successes including 'Blythe Spirit' and 'Oliver!', which was presented together with the children of the Stage School. Other productions were directed by Peter and John Skinner and John Dove. Their last production was 'Me and My Girl' in 1998.

Ken Dodd, September 1986, courtesy of Chad. Whatever the year - Ken Dodd's show is a guaranteed 'sell-out'!

In January 1984, Colin revived the professional pantomime at the Civic, with a production of 'Aladdin'. Colin Crompton, who appeared in the panto, wrote a sincere, personal note of thanks for helping to make his three-weeks in Mansfield both comfortable and enjoyable. He wrote 'After two years absence from the pantomime scene, I was half-expecting problems somewhere along the line but, thanks to you and your excellent staff, there were none.'

The success of these pantomimes gradually built up year after year, thanks to the hard work of all the staff, both full and part-time.

Nicholas Parsons, who appeared as 'Baron Hardup' - with Ruth Madoc as 'Prince Charming' - in the 1992-3 season of 'Cinderella', wrote a glowing article in the Daily Telegraph about his five week stay in the town and working with Colin and his staff.

The female impersonators, Hinge and Bracket, who came several times, always expressed their pleasure and delight in having a Victorian drawing-room set specially built for them.

Tommy Trinder, who appeared on-stage in 1980, disliked staying in hotels. He stayed with Jean Carter's sister and family, who found their lodger highly entertaining.

From April to September 1994, the Civic was closed for even more extensive refurbishing, in a £250,000 project financed by the District Council, with assistance from European Funding.

The dress circle of forty-seven seats, was extended to one hundred and fifty - this increased the capacity of the Theatre to six hundred. The improved sound system was located at the rear of the stalls, as was the lighting.

To comply with strict Health and Safety Regulations, a new fire alarm system and fire escape were installed. The auditorium was also completely redecorated.

In an article introducing the 'New Look', the Weekly Post and Recorder commented, **'The improvements and increased capacity, along with the Theatre's long standing reputation for attracting top stars, all contribute to the Civic being one of the best theatres in the Midlands'.**

This was borne out in the opening weekend when, on September 30th, Ken Dodd and his Laughter Show made a return visit. Other highlights of this season were Marti Webb, the Ronnie Scott Quartet, Sooty's Wild West Show and the popular poets Roger McGough and Pam Ayres.

Philip Hitchcock, nominated by the Magic Circle as 'Young Magician of the Year', had previously been in Barbara Windsor's 'Old Time Music Hall' at the Civic. He returned in December 1994 to take part in 'Dick Whittington' which starred Bob Carolgees as 'Idle Jack'. Philip became Colin and Jean's son-in-law when he married their daughter Jane, who worked backstage. Jane became Philip's assistant and for two years they toured all the major theatres in the country as part of Ken Dodd's 'Laughter Show'. Now a mother of three, Jane no longer appears on stage but Philip continues to thrill and baffle audiences with his magic, in the theatre and on cruise ships.

When Colin took early retirement in 1994, the Leisure Services Committee made a presentation and offered their appreciation for his years of dedicated service to the Civic. In his reply Colin thanked the Committee for its continued support and asked them not to lose sight of the feasibility study which had been carried out for the improvement of the backstage area. Jean Carter, who also worked backstage, is still well-remembered for the 'last night 'buffet parties which she put on for the cast, crew and friends.

After his retirement Colin continued to work at the Theatre for a few years, on a part time basis. He still misses all the wonderful people he met and worked with, particularly the backstage and technical crews and the part time staff.

The Civic Theatre Technical Staff

Theatre Manager	COLIN CARTER
Lighting Designer	MURRAY MACDONALD
Sound & Show Co-ordinator	JONATHAN D. NUTTALL
Wardrobe (Principals)	NORMA HUGHES
Wardrobe (Chorus)	LYNN NETTLESHIP
Technical Assistants (Stage)	MICK SAVAGE, EDDIE RATCLIFFE, DENNIS RANDALL, PHILLIP MORRIS, BRYON BARLOW, SIMON ROSTRON, DOUG GARDNER, JOSÉ COOK, CYRIL JOHNSON, ROBERT PILMORE, LEE ORRAL
Follow Spots	MATTHEW DAWSON, EMMA BARNETT, TINA POULSON, JONATHON BARLOW, DAVID SAVAGE, IAN SAVAGE, STEVEN GREY, ADRIAN JONES, LORRAINE CROFTS, SARAH OXLEY, BEN HUTCHINSON, JANINE SHARP, ALISON SHARP, NICK BIRCH, CRAIG ELLERBECK
Front of House Manager	ROGER BROWN
Assistant to Mr. Brown	MICHAEL MERRY
Box Office Management	LYNN LAMB, DO MYNARD
Stage Door Keeper	STAN SISSONS
Publicity & Programme	JONATHAN D. NUTTALL
Cleaners	MARY HICKMAN, LUCY BARGEET
Usherettes	GINA, MARY, IRIS, SUE, PAM
Bar Staff	KATH RATCLIFFE, VIOLET CUTTS

Rotary Club of Mansfield

The Rotary Club of Mansfield

One of the groups who regularly began hiring the Civic Theatre in the early days was The Rotary Club of Mansfield.

Members of the Rotary Club of Mansfield are dedicated to raising money for charity and helping in community projects. With this in mind they have long sponsored shows in the Theatre, the proceeds of which have always been devoted to charitable organisations.

For over thirty-two years they staged 'Senior Citizens Opportunity Knocks'. This evolved from a choir competition to become a concert and gave the older generation a stage on which to display their talents.

In 1974, Rotarian Canon Warburton of St. Peter's Church, turned his attention to the younger generation and the club hired the Civic Theatre to present a talent competition called 'Junior Showtime'. Since 1983, the organisation of this long running and highly successful annual event has been in the hands of Paul Bacon.

The 'juniors' aged seven to eighteen, are invited to apply for an audition. The talents they offer cover singing, dancing, instrument playing, acting, comedy and other areas of entertainment. Both individual and group performances are encouraged. Of the several hundred young people who take part in the heats, judges choose the best and twenty-five acts are selected to take part in the show which is still a major charitable event in the Rotary Club calendar.

The Lions Club of Mansfield

The example set by the Rotarians was later followed by the Mansfield Branch of the Lions International, who have members drawn from all walks of life and were formed in 1967. In September 1977, to raise awareness of their Club and the aims, they held a promotional meeting at the Civic Theatre. This was by invitation only and attracted a large audience.

From then on, the Lions used the Theatre on a regular basis to stage celebrity concerts designed to raise money for their work with, and for, disadvantaged people of all ages. The proceeds of their 1990 'Magic of Music' show was used to support the Duke of Edinburgh Award projects for the children of Yeoman Park School in Mansfield Woodhouse.

The late Ken Butcher, for many years the driving force behind the organisation of Lion events at the Theatre, staged his and the Lions' final show in 2003. This was a Grand Charity Concert which offered another evening of entertainment for Senior Citizens and again featured the Lisa Gail School of Dancing, and also the North Nottinghamshire Police Band.

SENIOR CITIZENS' CONCERT

WE SERVE

A special concert marking the 20th Anniversary of the Formation of the Mansfield Lions Club and 75 years of the Lions International. Senior Citizens are invited to join a variety of acts in celebratory mood. Bolsover Panharmonics and Okra Steel Band, Damian Mellor at the organ and Lisa Gail School of Dancing.

Tickets – Free – available from Lions Club Members/Civic Theatre
Presented by the Mansfield Lions Club

Lion's Senior Citizens' Concert October 1992

Although no longer presenting live shows, the Lions, now under the chairmanship of Terry Partridge, have continued to hold successful fund-raising events, mainly at Easter and Christmas.

The members of the Lions Club still strongly uphold their motto 'We Serve', by using the proceeds of these events to sponsor and support deserving causes in the Mansfield area.

The Mansfield Amateur Operatic and Dramatic Operatic Society

The Society was founded in 1905 by a band of enthusiasts. Their first opera was 'Maritania' which had seven principals and a chorus of twenty.

For many years productions were staged at the former Grand Theatre but in 1978 the theatre became the ABC, a triple-screen cinema (now a Riley's Snooker Hall) and a new home was found at the Civic Theatre.

By comparison with its old home, backstage accommodation was very limited but the situation improved in 1982, when more dressing rooms were added. As part of this refurbishment, the Society generously supplied an induction loop for the hard of hearing.

Roger Brown, now more than forty years a member of the Society, made his first appearance in 'Chu Chin Chow'(1968) and continued on stage until 'Hello Dolly' (2001).

Early in 1970, when this musical was in its seventh year on Broadway, the question was asked, 'Who will play 'Dolly' in 2001?' When Joy Barden played the title role in the Society's 1971 production of this musical, Roger remembers the same question being asked. By sheer coincidence, 'Hello Dolly' was the choice for 2001 when the lead was played by Patricia Pattison.

Pam Frith made her debut in 'Annie Get Your Gun'(1960) but her stage appearances began earlier than this when, as a child, she appeared in the Thorpe Hancock Dancing School displays at the Civic.

THE MERRY WIDOW

CAST IN ORDER OF APPEARANCE

MADAME ANNA GLAVARI (a wealthy widow)		**GINA BUTLER**
COUNT DANILO DANILOVITSCH (Pontevedrian attaché)		**TERRY SCATTERGOOD**
BARON ZETA (Pontevedrian Ambassador in Paris)		**RON HALLAM**
VALENCIENNE (Baron Zeta's wife)		**MARGARET PRESTON**
CAMILLE DE ROSILLION (a French Count)		**JIM HINCHLIFF**
NJEGUS (Baron Zeta's faithful factotum)		**MICHAEL MERRY**
CASCADA		**IAN CARR**
ST. BRIOCHE	(guests at the Embassy)	**BRIAN MITCHELL**
KROMOV (an attaché)		**ROBERT JARVIS**
OLGA (Kromov's wife)		**MARIAN SHEPPARD**
SYLVIA		**SHERYLL HARDY**
PRASKOVIA	(lady guests at the Embassy)	**JANET BOWMAN**
BOGDANOVITSCH		**LEN PARKER**
PRITSCH		**BERNARD BAILEY**

Grisettes — Lo-Lo, Do-Do, Jou-Jou, Frou-Frou, Clo-Clo, Margot, played by **Elizabeth Butler, Lisa Skinner, Judith Booker, Anne Martin, Denize Jones and Kathleen Ratcliffe.**

LADIES' CHORUS

GAIL BATEMAN	HELEN BLOCKLEY	CHRISTINE COOPER
ANGELA CARRINGTON	BARBARA COX	JUNE FELL
JOY JONES	MARGARET LOCK	SANDRA PAYTON
BRENDA PARKER	OLIVE REDFERN	JEAN RENSHAW
MAUREEN KENNEDY	PAULINE PALING	EILEEN STANLEY
JEAN WARD		

MEN'S CHORUS

GEORGE BRADBURY	ROGER BROWN	DEREK BUTLER
JOHN BELL	LIONEL CASTLE	JOHN FLANAGAN
JIM HANSON	BRIAN KEMP	LES LOUNDS
BARRY POXON		

PRODUCTION

Hon. producer	JACK TYLER
Assistant producer	JOY BARDEN
Hon. musical director	BARBARA CALE
Dancing mistress	JILLIAN B. BENSON
Business manager	JIM HINCHLIFF
Hon. stage manager	GILLIAN CHARLES
Hon. property manager	CYRIL JOHNSON
Hon. lighting manager	NEIL BUTLER
Hon. wardrobe mistress	
CONNIE HODGKINS	
Hon. prompt	MARY RADFORD
Hon. accompanist	JACK STEAD
Deputy accompanists	JOHN SELLARS
	DENNIS KITTS

ORCHESTRA

Piano	JACK STEAD
Violins	REG LEWIS
	GEORGE WASS
	DAVID COURT
	W. HAINSWORTH
Cello	JOHN LEANING
Bass	NORMAN TOFT
Clarinet	LORNA BAGGALEY
Flute	HILARY GREGSON
Horn	DAVID HINCE
Percussion	HAROLD JENNINGS

The society's first full production at the Civic, in March 1979, included many names which were already familiar to local audiences.

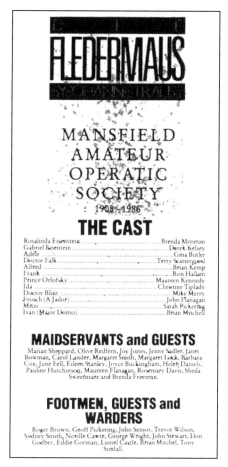

As Roger recalls in this 1986 production, the Society's leading man fell ill and a professional actor, Brian Kay, had to be called in to play the role of Gabriel Eisenstein.

When she was a member of the Masque Players, Leslie Orton gave her the chance to show that she could sing and act as well as dance, in their production 'Bye Bye Birdie' (1970).

Also as a founder member of the Masque Productions, among the many roles she played was 'Maria' in the twenty-fifth anniversary production of 'The Sound of Music', in which her daughter, Carolyn, played 'Brigitta Von Trapp'.

Over her years with the Operatic Society, Pam has taken part in many of its musical presentations but in 2001 she accepted a new challenge. 'Annie' (2009) was Pam's eighth show as Director/Producer. She was also credited as part of the Wardrobe Team and, with her husband, Norman, she was also Property Manager.

Pam says that, after more than fifty years working and performing in amateur theatre with such gifted and enthusiastic people, it is easy to see why she considers her 'hobby' to be so special and worthwhile.

Ian Hibbert's first contact with the Society was as an orchestral musician in the 1970's. Playing the flute and clarinet, he worked under Jack Domelow, Stephen Hepple and Barbara Cale. Ian has been involved with numerous musical events, including shows, concerts, operas, and gala evenings but, during this time, he never lost touch with the Society. He served on the committee and acted as Rehearsal Pianist. In its Centenary year (2005) he

71

became Musical Director of the Society, a post which he relinquished after his fifth show, 'Annie' (2009) - in which he also had a 'bit-part' as 'Announcer'.

Paul O' Leary, who has worked with a number of local companies took over from Ian. He was Musical Director for 'Oliver!'(2004) and 'The Music Man' (2010).

The Centenary year was marked with a special Sunday Gala Concert of a selection of songs from past shows. It was produced by Ken Cox and compèred by Leslie Orton, both of whom had long been associated with the Society. In the audience were local dignitaries and among other specially invited guests were many former members. The musical chosen for this special year was 'The King and I', in which Leslie Orton had, in 1963, played one of his most memorable roles.

When Roger Brown retired from stage work, he became Chairman, Ticket Secretary and part of the Front of House team. In his foreword to the 2009 production, which he dedicated to the memory of Michael Merry, a staunch member for over fifty years, Roger also offered his personal thanks to all who had been involved in the show, in particular Pam Frith, Ian Hibbard, Jenni Smedley and Katie Wright.

Jenni Smedley and her husband, Reg, both had previous experience with amateur dramatic groups and first took the stage with the Society in the 1980's. Since 1990, they have both devoted their time and talents to the 'Ops'. Jenni became Secretary in 2002 and still appears on the stage. Reg, now a non-performing member, still fulfils a vital role as the 'Secretary's Secretary'.

Katie Wright began dancing at the age of three with the Lorraine School of Dancing. She has danced with several amateur societies and, aged fifteen, began choreographing with local junior groups. In taking over the position as Choreographer to the Society, she is following in the distinguished footsteps of her former teacher, Jill Benson.

It is now over one hundred years since the Mansfield Operatic Society put on its first production and, apart from two breaks during the war years, it has continued to harness the talent and enthusiasm of the changing casts of players, to provide many happy evenings for thousands of local theatregoers and, each year since its inception, to give financial support to a chosen charity.

Mansfield Hospital's Theatre Troupe

Since they presented 'Aladdin' at the Civic Theatre in 1980, the Mansfield Hospital's Theatre Troupe have continued to offer their audiences a wide range of traditional pantomimes.

Several members have been with the Troupe since the very early days. One long standing member, well known for her comedy roles is Jill Broome. One of her latest was 'Queen Goosegog' in 'Mother Goose'. Bob Foreman's first show was in 1982. He has recently retired from performing and is currently Chairman.

Trevor Morley joined the Troupe in the same year as Bob and directed productions for fifteen years. He is now Treasurer, his wife, June, is Ticket Secretary and they both still appear on stage. Their son Chris, and daughter, Rachael, have both taken part in the annual panto's. Rachael has also been credited with designing programmes and posters.

Mother Goose & Off-Stage Cast

Scott McKenzie's first venture as Director was in the 2008 production of 'Snow White'. He combined this with also playing the 'Dame'.

The following year he both directed and played the title role in 'Mother Goose' as well as designing the programme cover. This was the ninth show to be choreographed by Jo Wilson.

The troupe is entirely self-supporting and relies on the continued support of many volunteers. Since 1980, the money raised by the dedication of its members has amounted to almost £100,000 and has been used to help charities as diverse as the 'Lincs and Notts Air Ambulance' and 'Riding Schools for the Disabled'.

The Troupe also asked local organisations to sponsor schools in the district. In return for this support the schools are given fifty tickets to enable the children to come along and enjoy the show.

In spite of ever rising costs, the members of the Mansfield Hospital's Theatre Troupe intend to carry on presenting traditional pantomimes with, as they say, 'the odd twist' to delight their audiences and make donations to deserving causes.

Roger Brown

Roger started his theatrical career playing chorus parts in Westfield Folkhouse pantomimes. At the Civic he also worked with the Penson Players, the Phoenix Players and in the Civic Theatre Company's production of 'Sweeny Todd', 'The Dresser' and 'The House of Bernarda Alba'. Having had previous front of house experience with amateur companies he joined the permanent staff of the Civic and became Front of House Manager, a post he held for over twenty years.

Roger has many vivid memories of the many top-line performers that he met during this time. These included musicians Humphrey Lyttleton, George Melly and Jools Holland, who arrived late and had to rush straight onto the stage and into his performance. When Eartha Kitt, the American singer, appeared in 1990, Roger had to deal with a slight disturbance outside the Theatre where a group of demonstrators were showing their disapproval of a fur coat Miss Kitt was wearing.

Among the many comedians Roger met were Tommy Trinder, Mike Reed, Jimmy Tarbuck, Max Bygraves, Frank Carson and Ken Dodd. On one of his many appearances in Mansfield, Ken, in his inimitable way, overran the afternoon performance to such an extent that the queue of people waiting for the second house stretched down Toothill Lane.

A great favourite of Roger and the rest of the Civic staff was Norman Wisdom, who came to the Theatre on two occasions in the 1990's.

The annual professional pantomime also brought many star attractions to the Theatre. In 'Puss in Boots' (1989) Norman Collier played 'Idle Jack', Clodagh Rodgers was 'Colin' the Principal Boy, and Sally Thomsett, well-known for her film role in the 'Railway Children', was the 'Princess'. Also featured were the Jill Benson Dancers.

Photo courtesy of Roger Brown
**Back row - José Cooke, Roger Brown, Mick Savage, Eddie Ratcliffe.
Front row - Colin Carter, Norman Wisdom, Jackie ?, Jonathan Nuttall.**

The 1990 season production of 'Babes in the Wood', starred Bernie Clifton as 'Simple Simon' and Rustie Lee as 'Nurse Twiggy' with Grotbags (Carol Lee Scott) as the 'Sheriff of Nottingham'. The choreographer was Jill Benson. Among the 'Babes' were Darren and Lisa Bottomore, Christoper Brown and Elizabeth Peacock. Among the 'Villagers' were Rachel Benson and Juliet Bacon. The following year, Larry Grayson, Mike Berry and Herol 'Bomber' Graham, the Nottingham-born boxing champion, took the leads in 'Aladdin'. Once again, Jill Benson was the choreographer and among the juvenile dancers were Lisa Bottomore, Caroline Skinner and Rebecca Price-Mear.

The year continued with such attractions as Danny La Rue in 'Privates on Parade', billed as a 'Smash Hit Comedy Musical'. Audiences were warned that 'this amazingly funny play contains explicit language and several scenes of nudity'. On a much less risqué note, were shows featuring the Syd Lawrence Orchestra and Jack Jones.

Included in the 1991 programme were 'Swan Lake', with the Vienna Festival Ballet, 'The Magic Flute', with the London Opera Players, and a celebrity concert which included William Walton's 'Facade', narrated by Richard Baker. Also appearing were Peter Skellern and Richard Stilgoe, Guy Mitchell, Kenny Ball and his Jazzmen, Acker Bilk and Humphrey Lyttleton.

The Cast

Simple Simon	Tom O'Connor
Jack	Denise Nolan
Bill, The King's Equerry	Tony Pitts
Dame Durden	Freddie Stevens
King	David Medina
Princess Sylvia	Jenny Dale
Fleshcreep, The Demon	Gareth Stevens
Fairy Godspell	Jose Cooke
Super Mario	As Himself
The Villagers	Lisa Gail Dancers

Also Featuring

Lisa Skinner and Chris Ponka

1994 - Jack and the Beanstalk Cast List

As Roger remembers the 'Beanstalk' caught fire during one of the performances. Fortunately, the flames were quickly put out and the show went on.

When Andrew Tucker was appointed General Manager of the Civic in December 1994, he brought with him a wealth of theatrical experience from South Africa.

After gaining a B.A. Degree in Dramatic Art, he worked first as Stage Manager, then Manager of the Theatre in Vereeniging, an industrial town in the Transvaal Province. Later, he became Director of the Theatre, a post which he occupied for ten years.

On moving to Natal, he became General Manager of the Playhouse; a five-theatre complex with an Opera House, Dramatic Theatre, Supper Theatre, Recording Studio, Experimental Studio Theatre and Function Rooms. Andrew then served on the Natal Performing Arts Council, as Deputy General Director.

Andrew Tucker - Palace Theatre Manager.

However the changing of financial support for the Arts in South Africa led to his resignation and transferral to England.

The Council had already decided that the Theatre needed a new name - one which would distance it from the anonymity of the word 'civic' and also avoid confusion between the Civic Theatre and the Civic Centre.

The short list of possibilities was published in the Chad and the public were asked to vote for their favourite. Of the twelve options given, six were associated with local hero, Robin Hood - Greenwood, Sherwood, Little John, Longbow, Maid Marion and Loxley. Others were Playhouse, Victoria, Byron, Everyman and Acorn.

Only the one remaining option suited Frank Kendall. With his strong and long-standing family connections, he had no doubts. In a letter to the Chad in March 1995, he declared:

'There is only one possible new name for the Civic Theatre and that is the Palace Theatre. The Palace Theatre has the right ring to it, as I'm sure many Mansfield people will agree'.

THEY DID

PART SIX

THE PALACE THEATRE
1995 - 2010

The name change, announced in April 1995, as a result of the Chad telephone poll, was only the first step in the re-birth of the Theatre. In 1996, a team of three, Iain Hook (Head of Leisure), Arthur Jephson (Business Support Manager) and Andrew Tucker put in a bid to Arts Council England (ACE), which agreed to fund £40,000 from National Lottery funds to finance a feasibility study which supported the Council's proposed £1.6 million grant. It was in January 1997, that ACE agreed to offer £1,630,471 towards the cost of continuing the upgrading, refurbishment and redevelopment of the public, disabled and technical facilities of the Theatre. This sum included the appointments of consultants and the payment of professional fees.

Owing to the increased costs in the interval between putting out tenders and the bid being approved, a second bid was submitted in order to make up the shortfall and in December 1997, ACE offered the Council a further sum of £129,420 from Lottery funds. This was to be used 'towards the capital costs of installing the counterweight system and essential technical equipment and to reinstate the artistic commissions, the air-conditioning control system and other desirable items, such as car-park surfacing, CCTV, dance studio improvements and improved finishes'.

In May 1997, the Palace closed its doors to the public and a seven-month period of extensive development began. During this time the Theatre was partially demolished, rebuilt and underwent a wide range of improvements which included:

- The creation of a sixty-foot high fly tower, to enable conventional backdrops to be used to full effect.
- The extension of the wing space, to enable an increased range of touring shows to be accommodated.
- The digging of an orchestra pit with an incorporated lift, that could accommodate more musicians and provide improved sound.
- The widening of the proscenium arch.
- The installation of a lift and ramp in the foyer to provide access to all front of house areas except the balcony.
- The installation of new seats to provide more leg room and comfort and to improve access for disabled persons.
- The refurbishment of the foyer, designed to reflect the Edwardian age of the building while blending with the modern environment, and providing a new confectionery kiosk and cloakroom.
- The installation of a computerised box office system, to facilitate a quicker and more efficient service for the public and to provide a marketing database for the Theatre.
- The refurbishment of the Upstairs Lounge and The Meeting Place, which provide the ability to undertake corporate entertainment, training and workshops.
- The new façade, which reflected the contemporary age.

Palace Theatre Foyer Staircase

This whole project cost around £2 million. In addition to the National Lottery award of £1.8 million, £64,673 was granted from European funding plus further investment from Mansfield District Council and on its completion, the Palace Theatre was re-designated as a regional mid-scale touring venue. It could now draw audiences both from the town and a much wider surrounding area. To complement the existing amateur and professional shows, there was also a broadening of the scope of performances on offer. These included classical music, opera and contemporary dance.

Delays in finishing these massive alterations caused the re-opening to be seven weeks later than planned. Unfortunately, this led to the cancellation of shows already booked for the original projected dates and the 'Sooty Show' being transferred to the Leisure Centre. However the curtain finally went up on the new-look Palace on December 15th 1997, with the family pantomime 'Mother Goose', starring children's T.V. presenter Peter Simon, which ran until January 10th 1998.

Over the following weeks, old favourites returned - Cantamus, the Westfield Folkhouse and Mansfield Hospital's Theatre Troupe panto's and the Lisa Gail School of Dance presentation. Among the theatrical firsts were Tara Arts with 'A Midsummer Night's Dream'.

The Palace celebrated its second season with a Gala Week (March 2nd - 7th) which included something for every taste – Opera, Classical Music, Comedy, Music and Dance.

This second season continued with a blend of the popular and by now traditional presentations by local groups of musicals, drama and dancing school displays. Alongside these, shows such as 'The Best of British Jazz', 'Give My Regards to Jolson', 'April in Paris' with the Hull Truck Theatre, and Wayne Dobson, with 'spell-binding illusions and hilarious

Palace Theatre - Light Sculpture

79

Palace Theatre during redevelopment

comedy'.

Two performances of 'Blood Brothers' by Willy Russell, was the result of four month's work with young people across the County and was the first of a new partnership between the Palace and the Nottinghamshire Education Committee.

Supported by the Mansfield and District Arts Association, 'The Music Collection', an evening performance of late 18th and early 19th century music was presented at the Museum and Art Gallery in March.

The Lottery Funding also allowed a 'light sculpture' to be commissioned. This neon interactive experience, switched on in September 1999, reacts to sounds on stage and in the auditorium. It presents a constant changing light display to brighten up Leeming Street as it can also be switched on to the 'street' position, reacting to traffic noises, when there is no stage performance.

With the Theatre redeveloped and offering an array of new facilities to increasing audience numbers, the grant enabled many other arts initiatives to be pursued.

Education and Outreach Team

A condition of the ACE Lottery funding was the creation of a part-time Education Officer. Lucia Hogg was appointed and soon showed that the amount of work far exceeded the available time of a part-time staff member.

Upon her departure, David Longford was next, but in a full-time capacity. When David left to move to the Nottingham Theatre Royal, Louise Wildish took over the reins. Louise was most adept at bidding for external funding and succeeded, for example, in obtaining over £80,000 for two years of education work which included Kevin Fegan as a Writer in Residence and Jayne Lewis as an Education Development Worker plus funding for numerous other projects. In 2005, Louise was promoted to Education Manager to oversee the increased responsibilities of the post. Christopher Neil succeeded her, joining the Palace team in 2009, and is continuing to move forward the work of the Education Team.

The Mansfield Palace Youth Theatre.

Throughout the year, children aged from five to eighteen work with professional Tutors to develop and gain experience in the performing arts. The students attend a class each week and work towards showing their skills in live performances.

In a year typical of the activities of the Youth Theatre, 2009, demonstrated the opportunities given to students to take to the stage.

In March, at the Old Library Theatre, Chapter 4 Youth Theatre Company (16 to 18 year olds) presented 'Grimm Tales' - adapted by Carol Ann Duffy and dramatised by Tim Supple.

In May, the Junior Theatre Group (5 -7 year olds) staged their unique version of Roald Dahl's 'Revolting Rhymes' - also in the Old Library Theatre. The second of their two performances was followed by an award ceremony in recognition of the children's progress throughout the year.

In June, the Intermediate Youth Theatre Company, Stage Left and Stage Right (8 to 12 year olds) performed their interpretation of Dahl's 'James and the Giant Peach' and 'Charlie and the Chocolate Factory'. This took place on the main stage of the Theatre.

Growing Bolder.

Growing Bolder, a participatory arts initiative for the over 60's, was set up in 2000 with funding from ACE and support from the District and County Councils. The project was aimed at promoting the benefits of life-long learning by offering courses at the Theatre, the Museum and in outreach centres across the district. Jayne Lewis co-ordinated their activities as part of her role of Development Worker.

Participants are encouraged to explore different art forms, both visual and performance, guided by professional workshop leaders, teachers and artists. Since its inception, many art forms have been covered – from creative writing to belly dancing, from drumming to photography, from glassmaking, singing and dancing to embroidery and theatre performance - and many more.

At the end of each course a sharing of achievements event is held before an invited audience. Throughout the summer, various workshops and cultural outings are also on offer. Partnership projects, such as intergenerational initiatives, have also taken place with other local organisations.

Left to right - Tutor: Mel Binch. Students: Joy Wright, Maddy Scott and Margaret Shooter.

The average age of participants is between 65 and 75 years, but the actual age range spans from 60 to people in their 90's, some of whom have been with Growing Bolder since its beginning. Over the years, there has been much positive feedback from participants.

Typical examples are 'Growing Bolder has allowed me to spread my wings in directions I hadn't expected' and 'I have made many new friends. One skill leads to another. You find out things about yourself you didn't realise you had in you.'

In 2005, several members who had enjoyed the poetry and prose writing courses decided to form an independent group, 'Grey Matters'. Their projects have involved writing and recording a radio play, producing a collection of comic sketches and the publication of a book, 'Holiday Memories' which went into a second edition.

Extracts from 'Holiday Memories' have been performed on stage in various locations, including the Music and Drama Festival and the International Day for Older People at County Hall. Their latest venture is a series of monologues which are intended for stage performance.

Another group of enthusiasts who decided to expand the skills gained in photography and creative computer courses with Growing Bolder are 'Bolder Vision'; self proclaimed 'happy snappers', with their former Tutor, Tracey Foster, they visit places of interest in the county, capturing scenery and moments in time, producing amazing shots and forming firm friendships.

Palace Community Theatre Company.

This group aims to provide adults with the opportunity to work alongside professional theatre staff to perform 'top quality' work.

Their inaugural performance, in June 2000, was the world première of East Midland's writer Michael Stewart's 'Questies', a surreal comic play concerning events at a Space Quest Convention.

The following year they presented another Michael Stewart world première' 'Burning', a suburban comedy played against the backdrop of Bonfire Night.

'Oil Patch Warriors', the story of Eakring Oil Wells and the American 'Roughnecks' who came to wartime Britain to drill for oil, was a play based on an idea by Janet Roberts, written by Phil Holmes and enacted by the Company in 2002.

'A Guinea Too Much' a new work by local writers Barry Heath and Karen Restaino, was the choice for 2003. The play explored life, poverty, love, lust and friendship in Victorian Mansfield.

'Wembley Ho', which focused on the 1987 Mansfield Town Football Club Wembley final for the Rover Freight Cup, was staged in September 2004.

David Hopkins wrote the 2005 production of 'The Songwriter' which was followed by 'A Site for Sore Eyes', especially commissioned from Kevin Fegan, and which concerned a derelict and haunted hospital, 'King's Hill'.

These productions had all been written by local people or commissioned by the Company but in 2007, with Becky Matter as Director, they accepted a new challenge and presented a classical text, Bertolt Brecht's 'The Caucasian Chalk Circle'. This trend continued with 'The Beaux Stratagem' by George Farquhar in 2008 and 'The Crucible' by Arthur Miller in 2009.

The Palace Community Theatre Company has continued to uphold its original aims. It is open to adults of all ages and background and regardless of previous experience.

This commitment has been shared by Joy Wright, who has appeared in every production since 2000 and who had no previous experience of acting. She says what she enjoys most is the camaraderie of her fellow enthusiasts and the thrill of performing before a live audience.

Working with Schools

The Palace has built up an excellent relationship with schools by providing a wide range of shows suitable for all aspects of the curriculum. A selection from the 2009 programme demonstrates the Theatre's commitment to this policy.

In February and presented by Scamp, there was a return 'sold out' presentation of 'Private Peaceful', a dramatisation of Michael Morpurgo's award-winning book which told a story of a young W.W.I soldier's final day. Although an evening performance, this educational link was offered at a reduced ticket rate for school bookings.

Presented in March, by Quantum, 'The Calculating Mr. One' was a lively musical comedy, linked to the Maths curriculum and aimed a Key Stage 2 pupils.

Also in March, 'How the Giraffe Got Its Neck', presented by Tall Stories, was a mixture of storytelling and science, suitable for everyone from the age of four upwards.

The popular 'Shakespeare 4 Kidz' returned in September with their musical adaptation of 'Macbeth', which was ideal for students of Key Stages 2 and 3.

In October, the Shakespeare for Schools Festival came to the Palace. Working in partnership with the National Theatre and the National Youth Theatre to support young people on their way to becoming professional Shakespearean players, the Festival gave four local schools the opportunity to stage four different half-hour plays.

Earlier in 2009, the Palace had commissioned the Samanya Theatre Company to deliver an active piece of theatre in primary schools. Following the success of this tour 'Sophia and the Magic Skirt', with storytelling, music and puppetry, was presented in the Old Library Theatre, this time for the public.

To end the year in traditional style, children from three to eight years old were treated to sessions of Christmas Storytelling in the Museum Bailey Gallery.

Working in the Community.

The Theatre continues to create projects and initiatives for the whole Community, working in partnership with many agencies, companies and organisations.

During 2009, and back by demand, ladies aged eighteen plus enjoyed three courses of Belly Dancing, for beginners and improvers with Cara Amirah as their Tutor. These included 'Exercise Through Dance' and 'Latin Solo' courses designed for the over-50's and led by Leanne Martin.

For those interested in the varied aspects of the theatrical profession a number of activities were offered throughout the year. 'Soap Scene', a two-hour workshop by ex-Emmerdale actress, Dee Whitehead, explored the reality of TV work. This was followed by 'The Black Box', a short season of workshops for aspiring playwrights, led by Kevin Fegan, who for two years had been funded by ACE to be Playwright in Residence. Kevin has written over forty stage plays, including 'When Frankenstein Came to Matlock'- especially for the Senior Youth Theatre and performed on the main stage - and 'The Forest' which was staged in the Old Library Theatre in 2008.

New Perspectives Artistic Director, Daniel Buckroyd, ran a day-long Directing Masterclass at the Old Library, and the Upstairs Lounge was the venue for 'Voice of an Actor' when Gary Lagden hosted a two-hour session with a view to enhancing vocal techniques.

The Upstairs Lounge was also the scene of an interactive Chinese Culture Workshop, directed by the Asian artiste, Ling Peng, which explored Chinese stories, songs and music. Ling Peng would return to celebrate the Chinese New Year, in February 2010, with lantern making, music and storytelling workshops for young people.

Another facet of working with the Community is 'On the Write Track' a series in which aspiring playwrights are offered an opportunity to create a studio play for the Palace Theatre. After submitting a sample script, two adult writers are chosen and work closely with Kevin Fegan, over a number of workshops, to create their own thirty minute play for two actors. These workshops culminate in a weekend with two professional actors and a script-in-hand presentation at the Old Library Theatre.

The Palace Theatre Music Society

A further significant step in the development of the Theatre's cultural life was in 1997 with the formation of the Palace Theatre Music Society. The Society is governed by an Executive Committee elected from and by its Members. Its aims are to organise and promote Classical Music, thereby extending people's enjoyment and understanding of it. The Society grew appreciatively in its first year, with members benefiting from the discounts for the Midweek Music Series held at the Museum.

Among one of the most notable early events in this long-running series was in April 1998 with 'Liszt Returns to Mansfield', with Robin and Kim Colevill re-creating the historic performance given by Liszt and his musical colleagues in Mansfield in September 1840.

Also in 1998, as a subscription offer, four tickets for the price of three were available to potential members for a season of four English Sinfonia Concerts. The highlight of the opening presentation was Rosauro's 'Marimba Concerto' performed by the international percussionist, Evelyn Glennie, OBE. This was a memorable 'first' for the Theatre – with a 90% house for orchestral music. Evelyn Glennie returned as guest soloist with the English Sinfonia in November 2000, as part of the Palace Classics III season.

Members, while continuing to receive the 20% discount offered on all concerts staged by the Society, also became entitled to a 10% discount on certain productions of a Classical nature - including ballet, operas and orchestral works.

In November 2006, the Society presented 'The Classic Buskers' with Michael Copley and Ian Moore, who both entertained and educated their audience in classical music with virtuosity and laughter at the Crescent Centre, Bull Farm. The move was made from the Museum as the Crescent Centre offered improved acoustics, better sight lines and has the same model grand piano as the Palace Theatre. This saves money on not having to move the Theatre's piano and reduces the risk to the instrument.

Since this time, the Society has continued to use the Crescent Centre as the venue for their varied programme of events which take place four times a year. There is always a piano recital in January to celebrate the birthday of John Ogdon. In 2009, this was performed by the award-winning Czech pianist, Libor Novacek. The Royal College of Music Brass Quartet appeared in September and, in November, the Society welcomed the Fujita Sisters who performed on cello and piano.

The Palace Theatre Music Society continues to remain faithful to its original aims.

Cultural Services beyond the Palace

With their Education and Outreach programmes, it can be seen that the Management of the Palace is not only committed to the management of the facility but, in having Andrew as the Cultural Services Manager, sees the role of the Theatre as a facilitator in making arts happen in Mansfield, and not only in the Palace. Hence they also work in the Old Library Theatre and the Crescent Centre, as well as in schools, and, most recently, in SureStart Drop-in Centres which provide opportunities for families and young people to meet up and try new things.

It became clear that the efforts of the team were being recognized not only in climbing audience numbers but also officially.

In 'A Word from the Management', in the August 2003 Brochure, Andrew was pleased to report:

'As you can well imagine, a lot of hard work takes place behind the scenes at a theatre and the Palace is no exception! It is important to be able to measure service levels and ability and in three recent assessments, the Theatre team has come out tops! The Theatre survived the District Council's Cultural Services Best Value inspection carried out by the government Audit Commission which concluded that we are 'a good service that has promising prospects for improvement.' This is the second highest score possible. The staff were also successfully re-awarded their 'Investors in People' accreditation. Finally the team retained their Hospitality Assured Award. We would also like to thank our ever-growing audience for its strong and continued support, and the positive comments and feedback that we receive. I hope you find much to amuse you and yours this season.'

'We're closer than you think!'

The new strap-line 'We're closer than you think' was introduced as it was evident that the Palace was drawing audiences from well beyond the borders of Mansfield. However, the perception existed that Mansfield and its Palace Theatre was 'a long way away' for those who did not live locally. The marketing campaign was designed to show that the reality was quite different and the road infrastructure to Mansfield from all directions was excellent.

Marketing Team

It is virtually impossible for a business to succeed in the present day without either having a captive market or a sensible marketing strategy.

To capture the 'Leisure Pound' is yet more difficult because it is a non-essential expenditure in a highly competitive market.

It was therefore not unexpected when ACE made it one of their conditions to be met before they awarded their Lottery-funded grant, the agreement to appoint a Marketing Manager with a suitable budget. There was also the understanding that the situation would be reviewed again with the intention of appointing a Marketing Assistant in the future.

Prior to the Lottery-funding, the marketing and publicity was not only restricted to what the Manager and his Clerical Assistant had been able to achieve in addition to their numerous other duties, but elementary technology such as a PC or fax machine was sadly lacking, even in 1996! There was no computerised database and the Tippex was always to hand to correct mistakes on the trusty 'golf ball' typewriter that Anne Griffin, the Theatre Clerk used. The ACE funding changed all that, provided the staff with individual computers, and a sophisticated Box Office ticketing and management information system.

Longstanding customers will remember the tiny cubicle that served as a Box Office for all those years. That was transformed into a more practical space that could simultaneously serve two customers at a time at the windows and another on the telephone.

The benefits of these improvements have been visible for all to see. Sam Hunt was the first Marketing Manager and she set up many of the systems that were to be developed and expanded upon. Communication with the media became rapid, diverse and frequent promoting the Palace well beyond the borders of Mansfield, drawing in customers from far and wide within the 40 minute drive time that the Theatre is marketed.

Upon Sam's departure, Louise Atkin was appointed and Louise has been instrumental in moving the Theatre on still further. A particular improvement has been in the quality of the seasonal brochures. This improvement of the brochures and publications has been recognised, with the Palace being awarded the Encore Magazine trophy for 'Best Venue Showguide in the Country' in December 2005.

Chad 24th May 2006
Louise Atkin with Best Venue Showguide Trophy

The Theatre now uses a range of media to communicate with its audience which includes billboards, bus adverts, specific media events, numerous publications, e-mail marketing and its website. The website is a powerful selling tool with annual page views increasing exponentially since the site was launched in 2007/8 to around 700,000 over 10 months in 2009/2010.

Lauren Whysall was a welcome addition as the long-awaited Marketing Assistant in 2009. Like many other similar-sized venues in smaller towns, the Palace schedules mainly one night shows and as a result the Marketing team continually has to promote a range of different productions each week as opposed to a larger venue in a city that may have the same show running for a week or more. The additional staff member helped greatly to get the posters turned around, leaflets distributed, press releases written and generally increase the ability to promote the shows effectively.

Other members of staff such as the Stage Door Keepers also assist when they can with mailouts, labelling and stuffing thousands of envelopes to help keep the marketing machine working.

Most importantly, as a result of the programming and pricing policies and the strategic marketing of the shows, theatre attendance has risen steadily since the refurbishment from around 78,000 to over 100,000 and has consistently retained an exceptionally high average attendance of around 71%, or 380 people per performance.

Stage Technical Team

Dai Evans has been at the Palace since October 1994, when he was appointed Assistant Technical Manager. A few months later, he was promoted to the post of Technical Manager with responsibility for all the technical resources of the Theatre which include the staff, the lighting, the sound and stage equipment.

His full time crew of three is made up of Assistant Technical Manager, Adam Owen and Technicians, Kirk Jackson and Joe Tutty.

The Palace presents many different productions each year and each one has its own particular technical requirements. Dai and his team are responsible for ensuring that these needs are fulfilled. Organisation and planning are vital in the smooth running of the technical operation of the Theatre and a great deal of work has to be carried out before the curtain can go up.

Production equipment is received at the loading bay towards the rear of the building. It is unloaded and the stage is set ready for the performance. In technical terms, this is called the 'get in' and the 'fit up'. When a production is finished a 'get out' takes place: production equipment is loaded out and the stage prepared for the next day.

In the Theatre, both backstage and front of house, Health and Safety regulations have to be strictly adhered to. Ensuring these are carried out is another important part of Dai's work and one for which he is very well qualified. One of the most challenging and interesting aspects of this is dealing with professional companies from abroad. Not only is there sometimes a language barrier but they have different work practices, and a much more relaxed attitude to Health and Safety procedures. Dai has to ensure that they conform to our way of doing things.

The number of hours put in by the team are extremely irregular, depending on the needs of the day – and no two days are the same. Except for a well-deserved summer break, they are kept busy all the year round, especially when there are several productions in one week and even more so when they are setting up for the annual professional pantomime. Dai who has experience and expertise in lighting, designs the lighting plots for these.

The crew's motto is 'Be prepared for anything and be prepared to do anything'. They are indeed adept at tackling jobs far beyond the technical nature of their department and enjoy the challenges and opportunities each production presents.

With around 100,000 people now visiting the Theatre each year, the seats and the auditorium carpets had worn out quicker than anticipated and needed to be replaced. Therefore in 2007, funded by the District Council, the Palace auditorium underwent a £100,000 revamp.

The stalls carpet, which had not been changed in the 1997 refurbishment, was replaced and new seats were fitted. Most importantly the auditorium was repainted, highlighting the beautiful ceiling and wall mouldings and using colours more in keeping with the period of the building.

Councillor Barry Answer, then Chairman of the Council, told the Chad 'There has been a sympathetic restoration and refurbishment and it has probably gone back to the traditional colours from when it was built in 1910.'

Andrew Tucker commented, 'One of the things that pleases me is that the features of the original architecture of the building have been highlighted, so that it is more of an exercise in restoration than a refurbishment.'

Councillor Kate Allsop, Portfolio Holder for Regeneration, added her tribute, **'Our Theatre is a gem at the heart of the district; the increasing audience figures prove this. By refurbishing the auditorium we are saying 'thank you' to the thousands of people, both local and from further afield, who supported the Theatre by coming along and enjoying the shows'.**

The Palace re-opened its doors for the Autumn season with a programme of old and new favourites, both amateur and professional, leading up to the panto 'Cinderella' with a welcome return of Jean Fergusson, once more playing 'Fairy Godmother', a role she had previously played in the 1995-6 production of 'Snow White'.

Another Box Office Record!

If you have purchased Theatre Tokens as a gift for a loved one, I'd like to thank you for contributing to our Box Office staff winning the prize for the best increase in sales of Theatre Tokens in the North of the country.

The period covered was 1st November to 31st December and compared sales in 2005 to 2006. The increase year on year was an impressive 68%.

Congratulations to the Box Office team and thank you, the customer, for your support and efforts in purchasing Theatre Tokens.

Please see the box on this page for full information.

Welcome

It seems we have hardly finished counting the almost 31,400 tickets sold from our record-breaking panto and here we are about to open bookings for the next one! Thanks to our delighted audiences, we managed a staggering 97% sold with Snow White and the Seven Dwarfs last year.

We know that is going to be a hard one to beat, but with your help we are going to try hard! Booking for this year's Christmas cracker - Cinderella – opens on Wednesday 18 April. So please tell everybody and let's get Cinders to the ball.

It is always exciting to be able to welcome companies and artists to the Palace for the first time. We are pleased to welcome Opus with "Tosca" and very differently, John Campbell performing the music of the legendary Jimi Hendrix in "Are You Experienced?". Three big names to look forward to are: The Joe Loss Orchestra and Singers, Elkie Brooks and William Roache, better known as Ken Barlow in Coronation Street.

It is also a pleasure to welcome back other favourites. Middle Ground Theatre Company return with the major popular drama – "Dial M for Murder" starring Faye Tozer (STEPS), James MacPherson (Taggart) and Tom Butcher (Doctors & The Bill).

If its lighter theatre you prefer, Checkout Girls is right up your aisle! From the writer of "Girls' Night" and "Girls Behind", Louise Roach has written another: an amusing and honest portrayal of life as a checkout girl.

School Inspector extraordinaire Gervase Phinn is likely to sell out at the beginning of May as is Ken Dodd at the end of the month. The queue for Ken's bookings will form early on Monday 16 April!

These are just some highlights, but there are plenty more from which to choose, from comedy to music and from adult to children's shows. There really is something for everybody at the Mansfield Palace Theatre.

Happy Theatre-going!

The programme for 2009 showed the distinct pattern of long-running local presentations which continue to attract large audiences to the Palace.

The year started with the Westfield Folkhouse and the Mansfield Hospital's Theatre Troupe ever-popular pantomimes.

Every February the Rotary Club of Mansfield stage the Grande Finale of their Junior Showtime talent competition.

The Mansfield Amateur Operatic and Dramatic Society and Masque Productions continue to delight theatregoers with their lavish musicals.

The Mansfield and District Music and Drama Festival is always an important event in the town's arts programme. Solo and small ensemble items are held at the Crescent Centre, while the Palace Theatre is used for larger groups and for the Sunday Concert which ends the Festival. Taking part in this are performers selected by the Management Committee and the finalists who are presented with their awards and trophies.

The Cantamus Girls' Choir and the Mansfield and District Male Voice Choir, both renowned far beyond their native town have, over the years, never failed to delight their audiences.

Tribute must also be paid here to the award winning Malcolm Lees Ladies' Choir. Since 1973 and always under the directorship of Malcolm, their annual Sunday evening concerts have been eagerly awaited, for, besides the choral singing, there was always something extra to entertain their audiences. Every concert was presented as a Celebration - another successful year of music making.

Sadly, very serious health problems forced Malcolm into retirement and on Sunday September 20th 2009, at the Palace Theatre, the final concert of the Malcolm Lees Ladies' Choir was staged. This moving tribute to a great man of music was hosted by his long-time friend, Mick Smith of BBC Nottingham Radio. The accompanist was John Sellers and the Conductor was former Cantamus soloist Daniella (née Hursthouse) Smith. Also featured were guest performances by members of Malcolm's talented family – his wife, Sylvia, their twin sons, Craig and Chris, and their twin grandsons, Christian and Jonah. As on so many occasions in the past, the Tribute concert was a 'Celebration' and 'a great evening of varied music'. The Malcolm Lees Ladies' Choir gave their loyal fans another evening not to be missed but 'missed' they undoubtedly will be by all their admirers.

One other significant fact which emerges from a review of the 2009 programme is the large number of Dancing Schools from Mansfield and surrounding districts, who find the Palace an ideal venue to showcase the talents of their students.

With ages ranging from very tiny tots to mature adults, every style of dance is featured in their public performances – from classical ballet, tap, Latin, hip-hop and ballroom through to rock and roll, disco, jazz and many more.

Although some groups are relative newcomers to the Palace stage, and none the less welcome for that, others now have many years of spectacular shows to their credit. The one with the longest connection to the Palace is undoubtedly the Benson Studio of Theatre Arts (formerly the Lorraine School of Dancing) which has been under the direction of Jill Benson since 1976. Jill herself began dancing at the age of three and became a teacher at the age of fifteen. One of Jill's former students, Rebecca Short, who is now Press and Public Relations

LORRAINE SCHOOL OF DANCING

ANNUAL DANCING DISPLAY

Civic Theatre, Mansfield
FRIDAY, MARCH 2nd 1979
Commence 7-15 p.m.

BALCONY 35p.   A   22

Proceeds to Charity

Officer at West Nottinghamshire College, has long treasured the ticket for a show in which she appeared.

Rebecca began studying ballet with Jill at a very early age and took part in several annual dancing displays. She remembers the excitement of dressing up, putting on make-up, waiting in the wings and the thrill of the last night which was 'Present Night'. While the young dancers waited anxiously for their turn, Mrs. Benson would hand out the gifts which their parents and grandparents had brought for them.

Since 1984, Jill has used the Palace Dance Studio for her classes. Now assisted by her daughter Rachel, and with a broader scope of activities, the Benson Studio of Performing Arts still has very close links with the Theatre. Its present-day students no doubt experience the same thrills as did Rebecca and as do all the other dancers who take part in the displays.

Alongside the many long-running amateur societies and dance schools, the Theatre has other valued and regular hirers such as:

Phil Bottomore who has been 'stage struck' since the age of five. In later life he joined several local amateur companies and appeared on the stage of the Theatre. Later still he got his Equity Card, turned professional and made several television appearances.

In 1992, after receiving a grant from the County Council, he studied at the Mountview Theatre School in London and, from 1995-8, he ran his own Theatre School in Sutton.

In 2001, Phil set up his own company, 'Far Out Productions', with a successful re-staging at the Palace of Barry Heath's 'Me Mam Sez' and 'Ya Shunta Joined', together with the

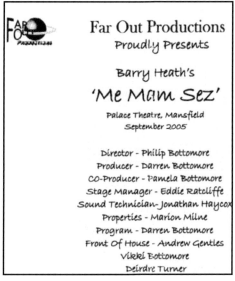

Far Out Productions
Proudly Presents

Barry Heath's
'Me Mam Sez'

Palace Theatre, Mansfield
September 2005

Director - Philip Bottomore
Producer - Darren Bottomore
Co-Producer - Pamela Bottomore
Stage Manager - Eddie Ratcliffe
Sound Technician - Jonathan Haycox
Properties - Marion Milne
Program - Darren Bottomore
Front Of House - Andrew Gentles
Vikki Bottomore
Deirdre Turner

second in this series 'Seaside or Bust'. This was followed by the staging of 'Blood Brothers' and " 'Allo 'Allo! "

The rest of Phil's family also have close connections with the acting profession and the Palace Theatre. His wife, Pam, a dance teacher, his son Darren and his daughter, Lisa, have all worked on the Front of House Team. Darren went on to study Theatre Management at Edinburgh University and Lisa not only appears in her Dad's plays but also directed the production of " 'Allo 'Allo! " Vikki, the youngest of the family, studied Theatre Arts at Derby University. She has been in every one of her Dad's productions.

With the continuing success of Far Out Productions, Phil and his family hope to continue entertaining audiences at the Palace, but Phil has decided to let go of the reins slightly and leave the next ventures in the capable hands of his daughters. This will give him more time to concentrate on his own professional career.

Royal British Legion

The Mansfield and District Branches of the Royal British Legion presented their first Festival of Remembrance at the Leisure Centre in November 1994. As it became increasingly clear that this venue was not suitable for either the participants or audience, the decision was taken to move the event to the Palace Theatre.

Since 2000 the Sunday afternoon programme has commenced with a Parade of the Union Flag and standards from the various Royal British Legion Branches in Nottinghamshire. The Navy, Army and Air Force Cadets, Associations connected with Ex-servicemen and Civil Organisations are also represented in the Muster. In 2009, two serving members of H.M. Forces; a Lance Corporal from the Royal Marines and a Craftsman from the Royal Electrical and Mechanical Engineers also took part.

A show of top entertainers, both local and national, follows the Muster. The afternoon ends with an inter-denominational service, during which thousands of poppies fall in memory of all the men and women who made the supreme sacrifice in both World Wars and all the conflicts since, including those which are still ongoing.

Yvette Price-Mear

Yvette Price-Mear's long-standing interest in theatre is so great she has compiled a 'Theatre Bible' of all the shows she has seen over the past twenty years, with the names of the actors and the roles they played. To date, it contains over 15,000 entries and, described as 'a unique example of audience memorabilia', it is currently on display at the Victoria and Albert Museum in London.

Every year since 2004, Yvette has hired the Palace to present a fund raising concert in aid of the Pet Bereavement Support Group, a registered charity which now also concerns itself with lost and stolen pets and re-housing pets whose owners are no longer able to look after them.

The show 'Mansfield by the Sea' has a different theme each year and is compèred by her daughter, Becky, who has worked as a Pontin's 'Blue Coat' and as resident entertainer at Blackpool Tower.

In a tribute to the Palace, Yvette writes, '**My husband and I go to theatres all over** the country at least a hundred times a year and we often remark that OUR Theatre compares most favourably, wherever we go, in every way. We are fortunate that the sheer range that is booked at the Palace, caters for every age and pocket. The welcome patrons receive from the Box Office and Front of House Staff is always very courteous and professional and, if one is fortunate to hire Theatre to put on a show, the service from the Administration, Marketing and Technical Management is truly second to none'.

The Family Connection

The Theatre functions as well as it does because of the dedication of its Staff, many of whom work as families in various capacities and have long term associations with it.

Lynn Lamb

In 1970 when Lynn started her working life at the Theatre, her mother, Mrs. Nell Worsley, had already been employed there as a full-time cleaner for eleven years and claimed to know every nook and cranny of the building.

Lynn worked alongside her mother as a relief cleaner until 1978, when she was given a full-time job. Later Lynn moved on to become an usherette, showing people to their seats and selling ice-cream in the intervals. In 1990 she was promoted to the Box Office, where she has remained ever since.

Lynn's memories of people and events in the life of the Theatre span over four decades; one of the most vivid memories is of the 'flood' of 1978. On the morning of Monday January 2nd, staff arrived to find under-stage dressing rooms already inundated by several feet of water which was still pouring in. According to the Water Board officials, an outside main and an inside heating pipe had burst simultaneously. While they set about locating and repairing the damage, which they suspected might have been caused by mining subsidence, the staff rallied round to work on the pumping out and mopping up operations. Carpets were hung on the stage to dry.

By Saturday, their hard work had paid off and final rehearsals for the Folkhouse pantomime 'Jack and the Beanstalk', were back on course. This ran from the week beginning January 7th and was a complete sell-out.

At this time Ralph Surgey, who had been employed by the Borough Council since 1950, was the Amenities Organiser in charge of bookings, publicity and advertising. One of his responsibilities was staging the annual Town Festival. Lynn remembers the special shows put on at the Theatre in connection with this – big bands, pop groups, operatic companies, well-known artists and local talent.

From the early days of helping her mother to the last twenty years working in the Box Office, Lynn has witnessed all the minor and major alterations, modification and refurbishments the Theatre has undergone. Lynn is due to retire in this Centenary year.

Kath, Eddie, Steven and Martin Ratcliffe

Kath started her dancing career at a very early age with Jill Benson, at the Lorraine School of Dancing. This led on to her performing in many of the Westfield Folkhouse pantomimes.

She has also danced with the Phoenix Players, Masque Productions, the Operatic Society and has choreographed for the Mansfield Hospital's Theatre Troupe.

In the Masque Productions 1979 staging of 'Grease', she was joined by Eddie who assisted with props and scenery - purely as a hobby. However, other theatrical interests soon developed; he served on the Committee of Masque Productions and is currently on the Committee of the Operatic Society. With Kath, he has been involved in the professional pantomimes at the Theatre. In the 1980's he was part of the backstage crew, where he still works part-time.

Eddie is employed in the Architects' Section of Mansfield District Council and since the 1980's has worked in the development of the Theatre, including the balcony extension and fly-tower, the refurbishment of the auditorium and, more recently, of the foyer.

Kath has also been on the Theatre staff since the 1990's and has done a wide variety of jobs. She has worked in the bar, as Follow-Spot Operator, Backstage and Front of House, where she now holds the post of Team Leader.

Also, when very young, their two sons, Steve and Martin, joined the Lorraine School of Dancing and both went on to work with several local amateur groups, as dancers and actors.

For Steven, the theatre is a hobby but his younger brother Martin, has had a passion for the performing arts since his childhood. His ambition was to become a professional dancer/performer and after completing a three year course at the Phil Winston Theatre Works Academy in Blackpool, he signed an eight-month contract as a production dancer on a Caribbean cruise liner.

'Scrooge', presented by Masque Productions in 2009, marked the thirtieth anniversary of Kath and Eddie's close and continuing links with the Theatre, first as the Civic and then the Palace.

Michael, Mandy, Ian and David Savage

Michael began working at the Civic Theatre in 1984. Previously he had been with the St. Lawrence Players, on the technical side of their productions. At the Civic, he was a part-time member of the stage crew and his work included building and moving sets and changing scenery. By 1990, he had been joined by his two sons, Ian and David, who worked on Follow-Spot Operators.

With her family spending so much time at the Theatre, Mandy also went along and made herself useful, filling in as prompt, working with front of house staff and making tea. David, who had been interested in acting since he was six, studied Theatre Art with Leslie Orton at Newark Technical College and made many stage appearances with local companies at the Old Library Theatre and, alfresco, at Goff's restaurant in Warsop.

Owing to work commitments, David is no longer active in the Theatre but his daughter Francis, carrying on the family tradition, is now with the Operatic Society. Both Michael and Ian are still working part-time on the stage crew and Mandy continues to make herself useful.

Jane and Michael Merry

It was the attraction of a free show, with contributions gratefully accepted, which first led Jane and a school friend through the doors of the Civic Hall. There, in the orchestra pit, a lady wearily plonking away at the keys, was trying to set a new piano-playing record.

Jane, who was doing some drama at school and was generally interested in the Theatre, met Leslie Orton who was in need of stage staff for the Masque Players. Jane volunteered to help and became the Prompter in the 1963 production of 'Salad Days'. She stayed with the group helping out backstage and front of house after school and later during her college vacations. It was here that she met Michael, her future husband.

In 1965, Jane went to see 'Damn Yankees' in which two members of her family appeared. Michael was also in the cast and from then on their friendship blossomed. They were married in 1967.

As well as being an active member of the Masque Players, Michael was also involved with several other flourishing amateur companies – the Sherwood Players, the Penson Players, the Phoenix Players, the Westfield Folkhouse and Masque Productions. He became an Honorary Member of the Mansfield Operatic Society, having missed only three productions, over a period of fifty years.

Jane supported her late husband in his busy amateur acting career and worked as Front of House Manager during the weeks when they performed at the Theatre.

Until his retirement, Michael was employed at the Palace as one of the Front of House Managers and, since 2000, Jane has also used her long experience and expertise in this important and multi-functional work as a Steward.

Little did schoolgirl Jane imagine that her first venture beyond the doors of the Civic would lead to such a close and still active participation in the theatrical life of her home town.

John and Rachael Street

John has worked at the Palace since 1992 as Stage Crew. His duties have included Follow-Spot and Flying, both with the older hemp ropes and the newer counterweight system. John's particular memory is of Cyril Johnson. Cyril, with many years of experience, was John's mentor and he learned most of his stagecraft from him. Unfortunately, with Cyril's death, we lost not only his wealth of experience but also his memories of the Theatre.

John's daughter, Rachael, has been involved with the Theatre since childhood. At the age of four she performed with Masque Productions in 'The Wiz' and has done more shows with this company. She has also performed with the Lisa Gail School of Dance. Aged seventeen and after her studies, Rachael returned to the Palace to work as Follow-Spot Operator, on the Stage Crew and, more recently, as Lighting Operator. Rachael's particular favourite time is Pantomime. She loves the fun and family atmosphere created backstage and the fact that everyone works together to make the show happen.

Both John and Rachael continue to work at the Palace as Casual Crew with the Technical Team.

Rebecca and Rob Pilmore

Rob has been involved in the Palace for about twenty-six years, working as Stage Crew and Flyman. Who would have thought that, many years later he would meet his future wife here?

Rebecca Pilmore (née Nadin) has worked at the Theatre for thirteen years. Her love for the theatre led her to gaining a B.A. Honours Degree in Theatre Studies - Stage Management. After university she returned to the Palace where she has fulfilled a range of roles including Follow-Spot Operator, Stage Crew member, Deputy Stage Manager, Lighting Operator and Box Office Assistant.

Rob and Rachael married in 2005 and had a son, Oscar, in January 2008.

Heather and Bob Hutchinson

In 1998, Heather started work as a Steward at the Palace, first on a casual basis and then on part-time contract. Her husband Charles, who is always known as Bob, came to the Theatre in 2003 as Cellar-man in Groucho's. He works on Friday mornings to clean the beer lines, take in deliveries and put everything in order for when the bar is open.

Since their hours are varied, it's not often they meet up at work, except when they both lend a hand behind the bar for, like other staff, Heather and Bob are ready and willing to tackle any task. Bob's not averse to doing a spot of painting and Heather used to be a waitress for pre-show meals when they were served in the Upstairs Lounge.

One of Heather's most enjoyable memories is of meeting Joe Pasquale on one of his visits to the Palace. It happened to be her birthday. The Cleaners bought her a bouquet and, knowing she was a fan of his, they asked Joe to present it to her backstage.

In Heather's opinion being a Steward at the Palace it is not just a job - for her it is a pleasure to come to work.

Gill and Anna Shewen

Gill started work at the Palace in 1994 and, with a short break, when her children were young, she has been there ever since. She now holds the responsible post of Senior Front of House Steward.

Her daughters, Anna and Rebecca, both studied dancing with Jill Benson and both appeared on stage with Jill's annual shows. Anna is now one of the Casual Stage Crew.

Of her work, she says, 'You never know what's going to happen next'. One such highly unexpected occasion was when the fire alarm sounded and they had to evacuate a full house of five-hundred and thirty-four people, in the middle of a pantomime. The highly trained staff did it in under four minutes. The exercise proved to be an excellent practice run for, thankfully, it turned out to be a false alarm.

In Gill's opinion working at the Palace is like having a second family and she is fortunate enough to be surrounded, not just by workmates, but by real friends.

Peggy, Nigel, Adam and Emily Gray

Peggy has been on the Front of House staff since 2003 but her connection with the Theatre started much earlier than this, when she studied at the Lorraine School of Dancing with Jill

Benson and stayed on helping with classes. Her daughter, Emily, now in her twenties, began studying with Jill at the age of three and, like her mother, she now works at the Palace on a casual basis, as part of the Backstage Crew. Nigel, Peggy's husband, also works backstage.

Like his father and younger sister, Adam was a member of Masque Productions – all three of the family appeared in 'Oliver!'. Jill Benson, who choreographed the production, started a class for the boy actors. Adam, who was then eleven years old, continued studying with Jill until he was eighteen.

One of Peggy's fondest memories is of the 2006/7 pantomime 'Snow White' in which Su Pollard appeared as the 'Wicked Queen'. In her honour, the 'star' dressing room was re-painted in Su's favourite colour and still remains 'Su Pollard Pink'. As always, the staff organise a party to welcome the panto players to the Theatre and Su, always very sociable, returned the compliment by arranging a buffet meal at a local restaurant and inviting the Palace staff to be her guests.

Peggy's work varies greatly, depending on what type of show is being staged, but she admits to loving her work and loving the Theatre.

Elaine, Jenni and Stuart Wharmby

Elaine joined the Palace team in 2003, replacing Anne Griffin who retired through ill health and who had worked for many years as Theatre Clerk.

Readily grasping the massive task of being Theatre Administrator, Elaine set about streamlining administrative systems, updating office equipment and setting in place labour- and money-saving initiatives.

Not being one who can sit by and wait to be instructed, Elaine is quick to use her initiative and to find solutions to a myriad of issues which the Theatre faces in the course of its activities.

Her daughter, Jenni, looks as though she is set to be a positive person like her mother. In breaks from her university studies, she has worked in a range of casual posts in the Theatre – from assisting with marketing, being a Follow-spot Operator and working in the Box Office.

Elaine's son, Stuart, has done his bit working as part of the Casual Crew for a couple of panto seasons.

Mansfield Palace Theatre Staff List as of 1st December 2009

Andrew and his dedicated team at the Palace are extremely proud of the Theatre and continually strive to do their best for the theatre-going community which they serve.

Administration
Cultural Services Manager   Andrew Tucker
Theatre Administrator   Elaine Wharmby

Cleaning Team
Caretaker   Paul O'Gorman
Cleaners   Julie Cornelly   Kevin Finlay
     Allison Knights

Education
Education Manager   Christopher Neil
Casual Education Assistant   Jodie James
Youth Theatre Administrator   Lisa Hopkinson
Youth Theatre Tutors   Jan Cox   Stacey Moon
     James Pacey   Samantha Penn
     Adam Pownall   Kate Reeve
     Marie Wragg

Front of House
Front of House Team Leader   Kath Ratcliffe
Senior Steward   Gill Shewen
Stewards   Jane Bingley   Bev Browne
     Lyn Cowley   Nellie Elenany
     Peggy Gray   Heather Hutchinson
     Jill Lowe   Dawn March
     Sue Martin

Groucho's Bar Supervisor   Julie Birch
Groucho's Bar Assistant   Gloria Hollis
Groucho's Cellar Worker   Bob Hutchinson

Marketing

Marketing Manager	Louise Atkin	
Marketing Assistant	Lauren Whysall	
Box Office Supervisor	Ian Grindle	
Box Office Clerk	Lynn Lamb	
Box Office Clerk	Marianne Watson	
Box Office Support	Jane Bingley	Mike Dawe
	Rebecca Pilmore	Jennifer Wharmby

Stage Door Keepers

Stage Door Keepers	Keith Bingley	Des Cox
	Alan Godber	Tony Green
Stage Door Keeper Support	Mike Evans	

Stage Technical

Technical Manager	Dai Evans	
Assistant Technical Manager	Adam Owen	
Technical Assistants	Kirk Jackson	Joe Tutty
Casual Crew	Ian Bramley	Tom Cauldwell
	Jamie Clarricoate	Kate Dovey
	Emily Gray	Nigel Gray
	Gemma Hoe	James Pemblington
	Rebecca Pilmore	Rob Pilmore
	Adam Pownall	Eddie Ratcliffe
	Martin Ratcliffe	Steven Ratcliffe
	Joe Salmon	Ian Savage
	Mick Savage	Anna Shewen
	Tom Slack	Daniel Stafford
	John Street	Rachael Street
	Owen Thornton	Shaun Tindall

They are guided by the following Mission Statement which very adequately sums up what they are setting out to do:

MISSION STATEMENT

'To provide a regional mid-scale touring theatre to be an accessible focal point for the entire local community and the surrounding area.

We will strive to maximise usage of the complex, promote lifelong learning and present a quality, balanced, professional programme across all genres whilst providing the opportunity for local artistic expression.'

. . . and finally . . .

The range of excellent mid-scale productions staged by nationally and internationally recognised companies has increased significantly since the refurbishment, reaching an all-time high in the Centenary Year.

Exceptional productions over the years that are worth noting are 'Junk' by Oxford Stage Company; 'Lord of the Flies' and 'Road' by Pilot Theatre Company; 'The Tempest' staged by Northern Broadsides and a magnificent 'Jane Eyre' by Shared Experience, prior to transferring to London's West End. Birmingham Stage Company brought a delightful adaptation of the children's classic, 'Jungle Book', direct from a London Christmas season. Northern Soul fans from around the county were delighted by the Urban Expansion's production of 'Once Upon a Time in Wigan'.

'Shakespeare 4 Kidz' have entertained and educated busloads of excited school children with their musical versions of the Bard's original works.

Hull Truck Theatre have graced the stage on various occasions, most recently with 'Beef' and 'Perfect Pitch', both plays by John Godber who directed their take on 'Frankenstein'.

Middle Ground Theatre Company have entertained audiences many times with plays as diverse as 'Dangerous Corner', 'Far From the Madding Crowd', 'Dial M for Murder' and 'Meeting Joe Strummer'.

Classical music lovers will have enjoyed the orchestral concerts performed by The English Sinfonia and Viva: The Orchestra of the East Midlands, as well as operas staged by Opera Box/Swansea City Opera, Mid Wales Opera and Pimlico Opera Company. A new and most welcome addition is Opera della Luna with their quirky productions of the classics.

Balletomanes were well served by touring productions of all the traditional ballets by Moscow Ballet La Classique, Ballet Ireland and European Ballet. Beautiful contemporary ballet has been presented by Independent Ballet Wales.

Popular music fans have been well catered for by a host of original artists such as Jools Holland, Joe Brown, Elkie Brooks, Marty Wilde, Joe Longthorne, Matt Monroe Junior, Dennis Lecorriere, Kate Rusby, Chas and Dave, Helen Shapiro, Rick Wakeman and Alan Price plus tribute acts too numerous to mention.

The variety acts now include the internationally acclaimed Chinese State Circus and for those of a stronger disposition, the Circus of Horrors!

Ken Dodd remains the most consistently popular artist to perform at the Palace with queues forming early in the morning and tickets selling out within the day. Other comedians who have thoroughly entertained the audiences include Joe Pasquale, Gervase Phinn, Pam Ayres, Paddy McGuiness, Lee Hurst, Dave Spikey, Jenny Éclair and Danny La Rue.

It would be remiss not to mention the exceptionally successful relationship developed with UK Productions who have produced the wonderful pantomimes annually since 2000, increasing the run to 62 virtually sold out performances over five raucous weeks.

Judging by the increasing audience numbers and popularity of the Theatre, it can be presumed they are getting something right.

The staff are delighted to be able to present what they hope will be a most exciting, varied and prestigious Centenary programme, commencing in January 2010.

They thank all their loyal customers for their support and hope they will encourage future generations to love, appreciate and value their Theatre.

They thank the dedicated local amateur theatre companies and dance schools for making use of the excellent facilities and thereby giving their members the opportunity to express themselves artistically.

And lastly, they thank the professional touring companies for bringing their work to Mansfield so that local residents can enjoy theatrical excellence on their doorstep!

MAY THE 'LEEMING LIGHT SHINE BRIGHT' FOR MANY, MANY YEARS TO COME . . .

Palace Theatre Auditorium